HOSTAGE/CRISIS NEGOTIATIONS

HOSTAGE/CRISIS NEGOTIATIONS

Lessons Learned from the Bad, the Mad, and the Sad

By

THOMAS STRENTZ, PH.D.

CHARLES C THOMAS • PUBLISHER, LTD.
Springfield • Illinois • U.S.A.

Published and Distributed Throughout the World by

CHARLES C THOMAS • PUBLISHER, LTD.
2600 South First Street
Springfield, Illinois 62704

ISBN 978-0-398-08869-9 (paper)
ISBN 978-0-398-08870-5 (ebook)

Library of Congress Catalog Card Number: 2012038139

With THOMAS BOOKS *careful attention is given to all details of manufacturing
and design. It is the Publisher's desire to present books that are satisfactory as to their
physical qualities and artistic possibilities and appropriate for their particular use.*
THOMAS BOOKS *will be true to those laws of quality that assure a good name
and good will.*

Printed in the United States of America
MM-R-3

Library of Congress Cataloging-in-Publication Data

Strentz, Thomas.
  Hostage/crisis negotiations : lessons learned from the bad, the mad,
and the sad / by Thomas Strentz.
    p. cm.
  Includes bibliographical references and index.
  ISBN 978-0-398-08869-9 (pbk.) -- ISBN 978-0-398-08870-5 (ebook)
  1. Hostage negotiations. 2. Crisis management. I. Title.

HV6595.S767 2013
362.88–dc23

                  2012038139

PREFACE

This book is the first edition of *Hostage/Crisis Negotiations: Lessons Learned from the Bad, the Mad, and the Sad.* My most favorite quote is from George Santayana who said, "Those who do not study their history are condemned to repeat it." In law enforcement and corrections, when we do not learn from our history, people die unnecessarily. With that quote in mind and some recent experiences at negotiation conferences, it was obvious that a text that focuses on lessons learned is long overdue. I have been involved in Hostage now called Crisis Negotiations since 1973. I designed, developed, and directed the FBI program at Quantico from 1975 to 1987. Back then the Federal Bureau of Investigation (FBI) followed the lead of the New York City Police Department (NYPD) in the development of a negotiations option to the resolution of a hostage or barricade crisis.

The NYPD was motivated by foresight. They understood that what happened at the 1972 Munich Olympics could have occurred in New York City with similar results. The FBI by hind-sight that came after a wrongful death suit known as *Downs v. US.* The incident occurred in September 1971. The case is discussed in Chapter 2. Briefly, during that hostage crisis, the FBI Special Agent in Charge (SAC) of the Jacksonville, FL, division assumed the duties of the On Scene commander, SWAT Commander, and Lone Negotiator. That is like playing the role of judge, defense attorney, and prosecuting attorney during a criminal trial. It is too much for one person to handle.

One could speculate that had the FBI acted to immediately correct that problem, Dr. Manfried Schriber, the police commander in Munich who, one year later, also assumed all three roles, might have learned from the FBI errors. However, J. Edgar Hoover was our director, the FBI had never been successfully sued, and we were all learning some new practices and procedures.

My problem is that, as I attend negotiator conferences around the country, I listen to case studies where negotiators present incidents and discuss what they learned. This idea really hit home with me when the FBI made a presentation on how sleep deprivation caused the negotiations team some serious problems. I remember well the Hanaffi Moslem siege during March 1977, when we used sleep deprivation against them. That case is discussed in Chapter 3. A short time after that, I was at another negotiator conference and attempted to discuss *Downs v. US* with some FBI negotiators. They had no knowledge of that landmark case known well to my generation of negotiators and every law enforcement and corrections negotiator I have met, taught, or spoken with over the last forty years.

Therefore, I wrote this book. Chapter 1 discusses some history of this process. This chapter also includes some guidelines on active listening skills (ALS). I firmly believe that a good negotiator, like a good interviewer, is not a good talker but listens well. We all know that negotiators and the negotiations process work best when we use a team. Team roles and responsibilities are discussed in some detail. The next three chapters deal with the types of folks negotiators are most likely to meet during a crisis. To make my points, I have included excerpts from the negotiator/subject dialogue.

Chapter 2, titled "The Bad" focuses on the criminals who typically take hostages. Basically they fall into two psychological categories: the person with an antisocial personality disorder (ASP) and the person who was labeled "inadequate" and now is most commonly labeled borderline. I discuss the two most common psychological defense mechanisms we encounter with them. They are rationalization and projection. To more effectively deal with such people, the negotiator must understand their thought processes. In addition, this chapter presents the infamous 1973 Stockholm Bank Robbery that gave birth to the term Stockholm Syndrome. Of all the cases discussed in this chapter, the one that best describes the person with an ASP is the Arizona prison siege.

Chapter 3 is titled "The Mad" because I discuss people who were or have since been diagnosed as suffering from a major mental disorder known as psychosis to psychologists and insane to correctional staff and law enforcement personnel. I discuss two of their most common symptoms; delusions and hallucinations.

Chapter 4 deals with suicidal subjects. They are the fastest growing category for crisis negotiation team calls. To better understand them, I discuss the issue of ambivalence. If they were totally determined to die, they would be dead before the team arrived. The question is does the person have enough ambivalence or indecision for us to use to convince them to come out? Finally it is important to understand that the courts in all of their rulings have not ordered us to succeed. However, we must make a reasonable effort to negotiate before the decision is made to "Go Tactical."

ACKNOWLEDGMENTS

As any author or negotiator will admit her or his efforts are never a single-person show. So it is with this text. Many fellow negotiators helped me get my facts straight for this book, and friends encouraged me to write about what I learned the hard way so others may benefit from my experiences, and in the process save a few lives and many careers.

I learned early in my FBI career that the Bureau was like the Navy. In the Navy, the Chief of Naval Operations is the boss. However, each captain of every ship is your real boss. In the FBI, the director, J. Edgar Hoover, was the boss. However, every Special Agent in Charge (SAC) ran his field office as his fiefdom. Between the SAC and Hoover there were assistant directors in charge of each division. Under Hoover, there were twelve assistant directors. If you will recall there was another leader who had twelve assistant directors. That, I think, encapsulates life in the Bureau when the new academy was being designed and built across the Potomac River in faraway Quantico, Virginia.

Geographically, the USMC Base in Quantico, Virginia, home pf the FBI Academy, is some fifty miles south of Washington, D.C., on I95. However, bureaucracies being what they are, those fifty miles may as well be an ocean. On our organizational chart, the Training Division is part of headquarters. However, in functioning and fact, it is quite separate. It is so separate today that agents stationed at Quantico do not qualify for the cost of living differential available to other headquarters staff who often live next door to each other. One drives north to Washington, D.C. and is paid the cost of living difference. The other drives south to Quantico and is denied this allowance.

In the beginning, Hoover decided that the computation for the number of offices for academy instructors in the new facility at Quantico would be based on each instructor lecturing forty hours a week and sharing his office with another instructor. Preparation would be done during his overtime. Of course those agents in the Training Division knew that lecturing forty hours a week was not logical. However, that was the rule of thumb, or in this case the rule of The Director. The number of instructors increased immediately under our new Director Clarence Kelly and the addition of university credit for most National Academy courses through the University of Virginia.

I say "his" and "he" because we did not hire our first female agent until a few weeks after The Director went to his reward. Interestingly enough, one was a former Roman Catholic Nun and the other a former USMC Captain. Interestingly enough every agent in the first Behavioral Science Unit was either a former marine or a Catholic. Some were both. As one of the first instructors transferred to the Training Division on April 1, 1972, I was told that should I ever meet The Director, I should not tell him I was a social worker or even a psychologist. I was a sociologist. So, for some six weeks between my promotion and his passing, I was a sociologist. It was never lost on me that I was the April Fool's joke on The Director.

The point of all this discussion is that many of the men under The Director, and especially those at the Academy put their careers on the line to do what was right. They said one thing but did another because they knew it was the right thing to do. Some call this cognitive dissonance. I call it courage. High on that list was Jim Cotter, AKA Inspector Cotter, who ran the National Academy Program. Jim, with the unofficial AKA of "The Dancing Bear" because of his stature and ability to dance around directives from D.C., won the Silver Star for downing a Japanese Zero with his .03 Rifle on December 7th, 1941.

Another WWII veteran was Jack Kirsch, whose grasp of reality and reading of men brought together those of us from diverse backgrounds to form the Behavioral Science Unit. During WWII Jack was a tail gunner on a B17 in the 15th Air Force. He flew dozens of missions over Europe and Germany. Though the men Jack brought in came from around the Bureau, six of the ten of us were former marines, two of whom served during the Korean War. In those days, the majority of Special Agents who had served in the military were former marines. That heritage served us well on the USMC Base at Quantico. Men like Jim and Jack constantly ran interference for us. They gave us the freedom to do our job as it should be done while they placated folks in Washington, D.C., with whatever stories they told that allowed us to maintain our focus and academic freedom. The mindset at Quantico was that our job was to help law-enforcement, corrections, and field agents do their jobs more effectivel,y not keep tabs on them or report them to headquarters.

In 1973, as the final decision in *Downs v. US* was being written, the call came from Director Kelley to the Behavioral Science Unit to formulate a better response to aircraft hijacking negotiations. This decision and case are discussed in Chapter 2. What we developed was quite different from the common practice in law enforcement, corrections, and certainly within the FBI in 1973.

Conrad Hassel, an attorney with a master's degree in criminology, is a former marine sergeant. In Korea he was in Baker Company of the 5th Marine Regiment in the First Marine Division. He earned the Purple Heart because early one morning he came too close to a Chinese hand grenade. Con fought organized crime in the Boston Division and the Ku Klux Klan (KKK) in Mississippi. As a member of the Los Angeles Field Division of the FBI, he is the only Special Agent who, with the help of the Coast Guard, boarded stolen vessel on the high seas, arrested the pirates, took command, and sailed it back to Long Beach. Con thought he was a hero. Unfortunately, reporters asked The Director about this before he was briefed, so instead Con was reprimanded. I am not sure how he was to write a report or even notify headquarters while sailing back to Long Beach harbor. Ah yes, life in a bureaucracy under The Director. Since his retirement, he won the Intelligence Star from the Central Intelligence Agency (CIA). He is the only FBI agent to be so honored and one of the few living recipients of that award.

Thanks to Jack, Con and I were selected to form what is now the Crisis Negotiations Unit. Prior to that formation, on July 1, 1976, while Con and I were in the Behavioral Science Unit, I began interviewing law enforcement negotiators to learn what worked. It became clear to me that what worked for them in a siege was what I was taught about how to conduct therapy with troubled patients. When I was in Fresno conducting a Profiling Course for the police, I went back to Fresno State and discussed this observation with my former instructors. They reminded me of what I had learned about listening. It became clear that most successful negotiators spent more time listening than talking. This tactic is called active listening and is presented in Chapter 1.

I learned active listening skills from Dr. Barbara Varley and other instructors at Fresno State and at the Atascadero State Hospital for the Sexual Psychopath in the mid-1960s. Unfortunately, we are still trying to teach this listening skill to law enforcement and correctional staff who are more accustom to giving orders, talking, and taking charge than to listening. Too many folks think *negotiations* is a synonym for *capitulation.*

In addition, it was obvious early on that just as the tactical, or SWAT element, required a team effort to do their job, we as negotiators also needed a team. Negotiation team structure and function are covered in Chapter 1.

In those days, the FBI was encountering hostage sieges on aircraft and in banks. Most of those on the tarmac involved people suffering from Paranoid Schizophrenia. That is the hostage takers not the passengers or the crew. In banks we typically encountered robbers who had an Antisocial or an Inadequate Personality Disorder. They are discussed in Chapter 2.

Because of the events at Munich in September 1972, we were concerned with terrorists' sieges. Those few we encountered did not require much of a change from the negotiation processes and procedures we developed for dealing with criminals. One such siege is covered in depth in Chapter 3. Today law enforcement negotiators are handling more and more suicidal subjects. These are discussed in Chapter 4.

With that background on the development of this life-saving process, it is important to remember that we are dealing with people and people change. Therefore, our responses must be kept current. To keep current, I have remained active in this field. I am a member of three state negotiator associations, Louisiana, Texas, and California. I am also the editor of the California Association of Hostage Negotiators quarterly newsletter. Because of my years of service and contributions to the field, I have been selected as an Honorary Life Member of the California and Louisiana associations, which means I do not have to pay dues.

Each year I am one of the experienced negotiators who judges correctional and law enforcement teams at the annual competition sponsored by Southwest Texas State University (SWTSU) in San Marcos. It has been run these many years by Dr. Wayman Mullins, who is the co-author with Dr. McMains of "The Bible" for negotiators, titled *Crisis Negotiations,* which is now in its fourth edition. He and Dr. Mike McMains have been my friends and inspiration for many years. They helped me with my first and second editions of *Psychological Aspects of Crisis Negotiations.* I call my efforts "The New Testament." They have also helped me with this text.

What little tactical knowledge I have comes from Dr. Tom Mijares–a retired SWAT Commander from the Detroit Police Department who is also on the staff at SWTSU. He is the co-author of *The Management of Police Specialized Tactical Units,* now in its second edition, and two other texts in press. He takes great delight in telling his audience that I was one of his instructors in negotiations when he was a young man on the Detroit P.D. I think he means that as a compliment.

John Sieh, recently retired from the U.S. Army Special Forces, has afforded me the opportunity to teach and train with him and his crew in the "States" and overseas in Kosovo and Tajikistan. In our state-side efforts and in developing countries, we focused on the need for close co-operation between his tactical and my negotiating elements during a hostage siege. Our instruction always concludes with a joint exercise. As a former "operator," John knows well the value of these elements training and then working together to successfully resolve a siege. We interpret success as rescuing the victims and capturing as many subjects alive as possible. Neither of us adheres to the expression "Kill them all and then let the Lord sort them out."

I should note that as an instructor at Quantico, I shared my office with Ed Kelso, a former Marine EOD (Explosive Ordnance Disposal) Officer, who was a "bomber." I learned enough about bombs from Ed to stay as far away from them as possible.

I taught for many years at LSU with George Bradford. We met during the Hanafi's Moslem Siege in Washington, D.C. that is presented in Chapter 3. Each time I taught with George, I learned something new. He retired from the Washington, D.C. Police Department as a lieutenant who was the commander of their SWAT and Negotiation teams. Max Howard, who retired from the FBI, was also active in this program and as a judge in San Marcos. Max has been a good friend and an excellent sounding board for me.

Bill Hogwood carefully reviewed the material in Chapter 3 on his siege and made several changes to my initial write-up. Sgt. Russ Moore, Detective Mike Rand, and Deputy Debbie Eglin from the San Diego Sheriffs office provided excellent information on some San Diego suicidal subjects and sieges discussed in Chapter 4.

Jan Dubina, retired from the Phoenix Police Department, was of great assistance and encouragement as I labored through the material on the Lewis Penitentiary Siege. She stressed the fact that the successful resolution of that siege was a team effort. I certainly hope my write-up conveys that fact. To make certain that this information is passed on, I will tell you here that more than thirty negotiators worked that two-week siege. They came from the Arizona Department of Corrections; the Arizona Department of Public Safety; the Maricopa County Sheriff's Office; the Glendale, Phoenix, and Tempe Police Departments; and the FBI sent negotiators from Phoenix, Quantico, San Diego, and Birmingham.

In addition, the FBI firearms staff at Quantico experimented with rifle shots through the same type of glass as they had in the tower. The cost of the glass was more than $50,000. The tests on the academy range convinced everyone that this siege, like that with the Hanafi's in Washington, D.C., had to be a negotiable incident. The resolution of that siege was indeed a team effort.

For two of the most recent cases presented in Chapter 4, I owe a special thanks to Sgt. Russ Moore, Detective Mike Rand, and Deputy Debbie Elgin for their efforts on scene and later reading my version of their efforts. In my judgment, the people of San Diego County are much safer because of the efforts and dedication of these dedicated public servants.

Certainly the pastors at my church, Pastors Carol and James Kniseley, continue to play a significant role in my life and my efforts to remain focused in my faith and work. Their sermons are consistently meaningful, and their service to our congregation is spiritually enriching. They are the embodiment of spiritual caregivers.

Without the assistance of my son, Steve, this book would not have any photos. Finally, to my Carole, who is gone from our earth but remains forever in my heart.

Thanks to everyone who helped me better serve those who call on us to assist those in peril and others in their quest for more effective ways to save lives.

CONTENTS

HOSTAGE/CRISIS NEGOTIATIONS

Chapter 1

THE BAD, THE MAD, AND THE SAD:
LESSONS LEARNED

The subtitle of this text tells it all. Typically those encountered by correctional and law enforcement crisis negotiators fall into one of three broad categories:

1. **The Bad** are those caught in criminal activity to include those motivated by escape, political, social, or religious protests. Psychologically, they tend to have Antisocial Personality and/or Inadequate Personality Disorders. They are not insane, psychotic, crazy, or nuts. They are self-serving people of every race, color, and creed who are criminals and whose life theme is "It's all about me."
2. **The Mad** includes those who are severely mentally ill and some motivated by political, social or religious delusions or issues. Typically, they are insane or psychotic and are experiencing hallucinations and delusions.
3. Finally, **the Sad** is a growing category of subjects* who are contemplating suicide. More simply said, these folks are criminals, crazies, and crestfallen.

In addition, **Crisis Negotiations** has replaced our first title of Hostage Negotiations because a growing majority of subjects with whom crisis negotiators deal are not holding hostages. They are lone

---

*In FBI parlance, the term *subject* refers to the criminal or focus of the investigation or siege. If I were a former NYPD officer, I would use the term *perpetrator*. Subject is shorter and easier to spell. Perhaps that is why the Bureau uses it.

suicidal subjects or barricaded gunmen. Certainly one could argue that any person who decides to confront dozens of heavily armed officers of the law is probably at some psychological level suicidal.

Many books have discussed crisis call outs from the perspective of the negotiator or tactical team. These sources will be identified when appropriate. This book will include excerpts of siege dialogue and discuss the "behind-the-scenes" efforts of those in the command post and other locations whose efforts and energies play an integral role in this life-saving process. Again, the goal of this process is the reservation of human life, not saving time, and money or taking revenge.

That said, there are times when the on-scene commander must make the difficult but necessary decision that to save lives a life must be taken. An example of this is the September 2010 siege at the Discovery Channel building in Silver Spring, Maryland, where a heavily armed gunman, who also had explosives in his backpack, took several employees hostage as he ranted on for hours about the station's role in overpopulating the earth. That's right; he was holding the Discovery Channel responsible for over populating our planet. Further, he was a repeat protester who, with each subsequent Silver Spring appearance, was more heavily armed, more vocal, or more intransigent. The bottom line is that his efforts were escalating. Escalation of repeat subjects is one of several signs that an on-scene commander must consider when making the difficult decision to use deadly force. This pattern of escalation will be discussed in this text as we have encountered it in aircraft hijackings.

There was a time in the early 1970s when the hijacking of an aircraft somewhere in the world occurred at the rate of almost two each week. In the United States the rate was just under one each week. For more than a decade we had the dubious distinction of leading the world in this category. For what it is worth, the FBI also led the world in taking hijackers into custody rather than killing them. This was the result of the on-scene commander carefully coordinating intelligence, negotiation and tactical efforts, options, and capabilities.

It is not the intent of this text to make light of a serious practice and process in corrections and law enforcement that has saved hundreds, if not thousands, of lives here and abroad. It is my intent to shed insight into a practical police and prison process that uses our tax dollars to save the lives of our fellow taxpayers.

For those who question the presentation of material that to some might seem sensitive, I will remind them that the process of Crisis Negotiations was initiated and is now a common practice designed and dedicated to saving lives. For those who read this book and seek insight into this life-saving process to outwit the authorities, I hasten to remind them that Crisis Negotiators strive to save lives. To accomplish this, we train and negotiate from a position of strength. That strength is provided by our tactical element. If one decides to play games and attempt to use this text to frustrate law enforcement and correctional negotiators then he or she will face the strength of our tactical elements; . . . they do not play games.

Crisis Negotiations Defined

Crisis negotiations is defined as a process designed to save the lives of responders, victims, civilians, and the subject. We take time to listen so the crisis can be resolved by bringing the subject to his senses, not necessarily to his knees. The key to successful negotiations is the proper use of time. Just as a surgeon delays an incision until the anesthetic has taken effect, so the crisis negotiator uses time to gather intelligence and fatigue the subject so that our tactical element can make a painless entry or ensure a painless exit that will save lives.

Who Am I?

With all that said, you should know that I have been in this business for almost forty years. Back in the early 1970s as a Special Agent, I designed, developed, and directed the FBI Hostage/Crisis Negotiations program at and from our Academy on the Marine Corps base at Quantico, Virginia, for eleven years.

My first full-time job was in the USMC. I served in and rose to the rank of sergeant at Camp Pendleton, California. I returned home and finished college. With a bachelor's degree, I worked as a social worker and then a social work supervisor with a master's degree in Social Work (MSW) from Fresno State. I worked in the Aid to Families with Dependent Children program at the Fresno County Department of Public Welfare from 1961 to 1968. My MSW program, two years long between 1964 and 1966, included classroom work and field placements or internships where I worked full time with paroles or patients under the close supervision of a carefully selected member of the staff. I served two internships, an Adult Parole Agent for the California Department of Corrections. The other was a Psychiatric Social Worker at the California Department of Mental Health hospital for the sexual psychopath at Atascadero, California.

I have included this brief biographical sketch so the reader will understand my background and with that knowledge put my comments and observations in perspective. Along those lines, for many years, I thought of myself as rather light hearted and inclined to see the humorous side of things. During my MSW years, I learned I was whimsical. Years later, while stationed at our academy in Quantico, I attended Virginia Commonwealth University (VCU), called by some during the Vietnam War "Viet Cong University," where after nine years of daily driving to and from Richmond, as I worked full time at the FBI Academy, I earned my doctorate. The topic of my dissertation was hostage survival.

On a more personal note, after I received my letter of acceptance from J. Edgar Hoover, my parents told me that at an early age, about five, I said I wanted to be a "G man." They thought that joining the FBI was a lofty goal for a preschooler. What I meant was a garbage man. I was very impressed with them because, back in those pre- and early World War II days, they drove teams of horses pulling large open refuse wagons in our Chicago alley. Their command and control of those powerful animals certainly made an impression on me.

It is of personal interest to me that early in life I was talking about working at a job that was important and required some skill. Frankly, I think most kids talk about their adult ambitions, in one form or another. That is normal. However, and as you will read in my chapter titled "The Bad," there are those, typically folks who have an Antisocial Personality Disorder, whose focus is quite different. One of my patients at Atascadero said, when teased about wanting to kiss his kindergarten teacher, he would have to kill her first. So, I was dreaming and talking about working while he was fantasizing about killing. Heredity, environment, or demonic possession, no one knows for sure. In the case of my former patient, I think one can make a strong case for a combination of the three.

Some Short History from Harpers Ferry

George Santayana is credited with the observation that those who do not study their history are condemned to repeat it (Santayana, 1905). I might add that unless you know where you have been and how you got where you are, you cannot correctly comprehend current events, intelligently consider the options available in the present crisis, or plan your next more or for the future to save lives and avoid civil court. Obviously, George Santayana is more eloquent and succinct.

The practice in the United States of negotiating with people holding hostages can be traced back to Harpers Ferry and the crusade of John Brown in October 1859. Brown and his followers were intent on stealing weapons from the U.S. Arsenal at Harpers Ferry and then fermenting an uprising, some say rebellion, of slaves in what was then the state of Virginia. Because of the quick response of the locals, his grandiose, some say paranoid, plan of theft and escape was thwarted. He ended up with a few dozen hostages, including a relative of George Washington, near the front gate in the facility's fire station that was called The Engine House.

The initial tactical response originated from the townspeople. Harpers Ferry was a blue-collar factory town. Directly across the street from the fire station hostage site was a tavern. It was well-constructed and provided excellent cover and concealment for those who chose to challenge the invaders. The problem was that they took a shot at them followed by a shot for themselves. After several rounds of such shots, some took it upon themselves to assault. They were shot, this time with bullets not booze, and fell.

The mayhem continued with a more organized tactical response from the Maryland militia. Among other things, they arranged for a truce and the removal of wounded warriors from the field. Some thirty hours into the siege, a contingent of marines arrived via rail from their Washington, D.C., barracks at 8th and "I." They were the tactical element under the immediate command of Lt. Israel Green, USMC. The on-scene commander was Colonel Robert E. Lee of the U.S. Army. His negotiator was Lt. JEB Stuart, also of the U.S. Army. You may recall from your high school history that Lt. Stuart was a cavalry officer, and you may think the temperament and training of a cavalry officer is probably ill suited to the protracted practice and patient process of hostage/crisis negotiations. However, Lee had to play the hand he was dealt. Due more to the intransigence of John Brown than the negotiating skills or lack thereof of JEB Stuart, the siege ended with a hostage rescue by the marines. The marines injured none of the hostages. Some of Brown's followers were killed, as was one marine, Private Quinn. Another marine, Private Rupert, was wounded. All of the hostages were rescued. Brown survived. He was tried, convicted, and hanged for his efforts. Was Brown psychotic or a patriot? He may have been a little of both. The debate continues.

My motive for mentioning this bit of history here is the value expressed and the precedent set by Robert E. Lee in the fall of 1859. As an American, he knew the value we place on human life. When the decision was made to assault and rescue the hostages, Lee ordered the marines through Lt. Green to unload their rifles and affix their bayonets. He did not want to unnecessarily endanger innocent hostages.

What Lee did in 1859 is the standard to which the courts hold commanders today. Simply stated, whatever course of action the on-scene commander selects, it must be grounded in the belief that of all the options available, assault, tear gas, sniper fire, negotiating, or some combination of these four or others, the one selected is most likely to save the greatest number of lives. Note the focus of the court is the saving of lives not saving time or money. Most Americans and our court system, but not all on-scene commanders, consider first trying to negotiate a commonsense response. However, this value is not universally shared.

Soviet Standard Operating Procedure

A dramatic example of the lack of value placed on the lives of hostages is the Russian termination of the Moscow Dubrovka theatre siege in October 2002. Briefly, a few dozen terrorists seized the Dubrovka theatre and held more than three hundred people hostage. As part of the perimeter security, the theatre was ringed with dump trucks. The drivers parked their trucks around the building to secure the inner perimeter and deflect any shots coming from those inside. However, once parked, they took the truck keys and left.

After three days of discussions, not negotiations, lethal gas was introduced into the heating system that resulted in the deaths of more than one hundred hostages. To further complicate matters, the local hospitals were not told what type of gas was used. Thus, they could not effectively treat the surviving hostages who were evacuated through the perimeter of bumper-to-bumper dump trucks into ambulances that could not get close to the theatre. Most of the hostages who survived the initial gassing died in the ER. The antidote, though available, could not be identified because the on-scene commander decided against the release of the identity of the gas used to the hospital treatment teams.

Further, the terrorists who were unconscious but survived the gas were summarily shot and killed by the Russian tactical team. Finally, there is the fact that the Russian people, according to their not so free press, considered this a victory for the government. Their not so free press stated they paid little attention to the unnecessary deaths of more than a hundred of their fellow citizens who were hostages of the terrorists and survived only to be killed by their government. There are other foreign examples, but I think you get the picture. We value our citizens. Dictatorships, unlike democracies, do not.

Each time I return home from abroad, I say a prayer of thanks that I had the good sense to be born in the United States. In democratic nations, people are important. The preservation of human life during any police or correctional confrontation is a paramount democratic consideration. I stress democratic society because our value is certainly shared by the British, German, and other Western European nations and most certainly by our distant cousins in Australia and New Zealand. I have worked and taught in these nations. I know from on-scene experience that this value is the foundation of our common democratic heritage.

The U.S. Precedent

To put this process into perspective, a short trip into the recent past is in order. Most people have heard of the September 1971 prison riot in Attica, New York, and the September 1972 massacre at Munich. Few know about the FBI debacle at the main airport in Jacksonville, Florida, in September 1971.

Briefly, in October 1971, the FBI mishandled a domestic dispute that began in Nashville, Tennessee, continued on a hijacked private aircraft, and ended in Jacksonville. Three people died, two of them unnecessarily at the hands of the estranged husband/hijacker. He then killed himself. We were sued in federal court, we lost on appeal, and I ended up with a career in crisis negotiations. If you are interested in the specifics of this case, it is known as *Downs v. US* (382 F supp. 752, 1971). It is also covered in more detail in just about every text on hostage negotiations.

In the Beginning

The credit for the initial design of the present police and corrections crisis negotiations process must go to the New York City Police Department (NYPD). After Munich, two of their officers, then Sgt. Harvey Schlossberg and Sgt. Frank Bolz, created and ran that program. Harvey had a PhD in clinical psychology. I do not know what that tells you about the pay for clinical psychologists in New York versus the pay for NYPD sergeants, but a doctor he was. With his background in law enforcement and his advanced degree, he and Sergeant Frank Bolz designed, developed, and ran the first hostage negotiations program in the world. Frank says that he earned his BA with the honor of Magna Cum Regularis. It took him sixteen years of regular attendance at John Jay University, but he made it. His is an excellent example of the positive use of time. Frank took his time to earn his degree as he took time to resolve a hostage siege.

Unlike most law enforcement and correctional responses, those sieges involving hostages are not necessarily time-sensitive. Dynamic inactivity, the positive and productive use of time to exhaust the subject while the position of the authorities grows stronger, is an excellent, effective, and court-approved tactic. Unfortunately, too many on-scene commanders operate as if they are being paid by the job not the hour, and they select the quickest resolution over one that is more likely to save lives. These lives include those of the hostages, the officers involved, and that of the subject. This theme, the positive use of time, will surface over and over again in my discussion of sieges. It is the primary topic and title of the book by Gary Noesner, *Stalling for Time* (Noesner, 2010).

The NYPD hostage negotiations program at Floyd Bennett Field began in the spring of 1973. The command staff of the NYPD understood that what happened in Munich the previous September could have occurred in Miami, Minneapolis, or any other U.S. city, including New York, with similar results. The FBI was so impressed with the NYPD program that agents from the New York Division and Quantico attended their courses.

To put events in historical perspective, J. Edgar Hoover died on May 2, 1972. By the spring of 1973, the FBI was secure enough in its strengths to understand that we did not know everything. We were so impressed with the NYPD program that we brought Frank down to Quantico to make a presentation. To this day, Frank insists that the FBI came up to Floyd Bennett Field and stole his material. That just isn't true. We brought him to Quantico, wined and dined him, and borrowed his material. Since then Frank Bolz has lectured at Quantico more than any other law enforcement officer. Because of his commonsense approach to crisis negotiations, he is known around the FBI Academy as "Frank Nuts and Bolts."

In those days, the Bureau was facing hostage crisis on a regular basis in banks and on hijacked aircraft. We have since brought aircraft hijacking to heel. Back in those early days, aircraft hijacking was a major concern. We were busy negotiating with people who chose to steal or borrow U.S. registered airplanes. We had a few incidents where the hijackers claimed to be terrorists, less than a dozen that involved criminals trying to extort money and a few hundred folks who were insane. Thanks to the Federal Aviation Administration (FAA) and the FBI in a joint program with the aviation industry known as "The Common Strategy," the hijacking of aircraft today is a rare event.

By way of example, between 1968 and 1972, there were 147 hijackings of U.S. registered aircraft. That totals one every other week. In addition, there were hundreds of bank hostage sieges. The Behavioral Science Unit (BSU) was ordered by then Director Clarence Kelley to develop a better response to a siege than we exhibited in Jacksonville in the fall of 1971. Since there was no point in reinventing the wheel, we took the NYPD program and modified it to suit our needs. Further, part of the congressional mandate to the FBI was to train police. We included hostage negotiation training for our agents and police into our BSU program that eventually spread around the world. Again, it began with Frank and Harvey and the foresight of the NYPD in 1973. To use a football analogy, the FBI scored the winning touch down by catching a pass thrown by the NYPD.

I reviewed the NYPD findings and principles and modified them to meet the needs of the Bureau. Conrad V. Hassel and I created the FBI Crisis Response Unit from the BSU under the name of Terrorist Research and Management Staff (TRAMS) on July 1, 1976. Someone figured out that *trams* was *smart* spelled backward, so not wanting to be the opposite of smart, the name was changed to Special Operations and Research Unit. It has been changed several times since. It is now known as the Crisis Response Unit.

I began the process of designing, developing, and directing the FBI two-week hostage negotiations program. To do so, I interviewed dozens of negotiators, hostages, and any hostage takers. During these interviews, it became obvious that what I had learned about crisis intervention and interviewing with emotional people in a clinical setting at Fresno State applied to sieges in prison and on the street. I knew the therapeutic approach to people with personality disorders, those suffering from a psychosis, and suicidal patients. During my many interviews, it became clear that what worked for me in therapy sessions also had application to the street. Basically, it boiled down to defusing emotion by letting people tell their story, also known as active listening. This process is discussed later in this chapter and in my book, *Psychological Aspects of Crisis Negotiations* (1st and 2nd editions) (Strentz, 2006, 2012).

Preservation versus Promptness

While the value of human life is paramount to police, it is not always the first priority of others observing or involved. As an example, I recall an incident near Washington, D.C. To set the stage, well over a million people work in our nation's capital. Most of them live in the states of Maryland or Virginia. Those who commute from Virginia are limited in their choice of routes because they must cross the Potomac River. This results in thousands of vehicles funneling from several streets onto a few bridges. The bridge that carries traffic from I95 is referred to as the north end of the world's longest parking lot. It was on one of these bridges that a disgruntled or deranged morning commuter took his car pool hostage. The responses from the Washington, D.C. and U.S. Park Police departments were excellent. They isolated the victim vehicle and negotiated a peaceful settlement. This effort took time, but no one was killed or physically injured. Unfortunately, this process required the blocking of traffic on the main artery, I95, for hours. The U.S. Park Police, the Alexandria and Arlington Police Departments, and other jurisdictions redirected most of the traffic onto other bridges. But delays for every commuter were much longer than usual.

Over the next few days, the *Washington Post* was filled with letters to the editor from dozens of delayed, disgruntled, and dedicated civil servants. The sum and substance of these letters did not commend the police for their excellent work. They condemned them for ruining their day and ruining their record of prompt arrival at work. They strongly suggested that the responsible party should have been quickly shot so their commute could continue unabated. In short, the commuters were more concerned with their delayed arrival at work than the lives of those held hostage. Often negotiators who, while speaking with a suicidal person, are taunted by citizens who are yelling at the troubled person to jump can tell a similar story.

Some of the lessons learned include the importance of isolating the scene by moving the perimeters as far away from the subject as manpower will permit. Once again, the positive use of protracted time versus the value of human life surfaced as an issue in the on-scene commander's decision to seek a peaceful resolution to a siege.

Listening

It is interesting for those of us who have been involved in this program and process since the early 1970s that the tactics and techniques we developed to deal with terrorists have such a wide application. Of all the approaches, the one that has the most universal application is active listening. Contrary to popular belief and media representations, a good negotiator is a good listener not necessarily a good talker. We learn when we listen. As we listen we learn. As negotiators we listen for the words, phrases, what is said, what isn't, as well as the subject's version of reality. This tells us how to best extricate him or her from this self-created crisis that is their present and dangerous dilemma.

Remember, the good Lord gave us a mouth we can shut and two ears we cannot. Perhaps there is a message from the Almighty in this fact of anatomy. In this endeavor, we have our team and especially the secondary negotiator to help us listen. Typically, the subjects we encounter during a hostage crisis have a story to tell. Effective negotiating teams pay close attention to this story. To help them tell their story, their version of reality, negotiators engage in the use of active listening skills (ALS). Typically, this story involves their version of events in which they portray themselves as, and believe they are, the victim. Typically, as negotiators, we are dealing with a subject who thinks he or she is the victim. This is crucial and must be fully understood by anyone dealing with a person or people in crisis. Forget reality. Reality is now in the eyes and mind of the subject.

Active Listening

The term *active listening* has been around since the years immediately following World War II. As I recall it originated with Dr. Carl Rogers and his approach to treatment that he called patient-centered therapy. The point is that this process has been around for many years. It is simple and it works. It is especially effective in emotionally charged situations and with emotionally upset people who have a story to tell.

My definition of ALS is doing something to encourage the other person to do most of the talking. That means we engage in activity to induce and produce more listening content. We learn when we listen. One of the best negotiating teams I have ever encountered is that of the Louisiana State Police. They strive for 80–20. That is, the subject talks for 80% of the time while the negotiator talks for 20%. They have a sign with 80/20 on it to remind the primary negotiator of this life-saving procedure.

Emotionally driven people will tell you what they want to hear from you as they talk about their perception of the situation. In all honesty and candor, I learned this from my wife. I knew that if I kept my mouth shut while she "vented," she would provide me with the answers she wanted to hear. Typically, people in crisis want to talk about their stress and stressors. Remember, the good Lord gave us one mouth we can close and two ears we cannot. I know from experience, there is a message in those facts of human anatomy. I have said this twice. I hope the reader gets the message from this purposeful redundancy.

The Mechanics of ALS

The process of active listening is multifaceted, but you need not use all of them.

I. **Tolerate silence**. When the other person finishes talking, say nothing. Wait for him or her to continue with his or her train of thought.

II. If you are uncomfortable and cannot sit and wait, **repeat** the last few words of what he or she said.

III. If you are more comfortable with **emotional labeling**, tell the person how he or she sounds—angry, depressed, etc.

IV. **Summarize or paraphrase** what the person has have said.

V. Ask **open-ended questions**. Do not solicit or encourage yes and no objective responses.

VI. Use **minimal encouragers** like when? Really. Oh. Then what?

VII. Use **"I" messages** like "I feel uneasy when you talk like that." This phrase can be used when the subject is emotional and yelling.

I have difficulty using "I" messages. Further, I have yet to be involved in an interview, therapy session, negotiation, or any therapy or negotiation session where anyone used all seven tactics. However, almost every session will allow for the use of silence, repeating the last word or words, summarizing, and open-ended questions. Open-ended questions are, in my judgment, the most effective in drawing people out.

By way of example, I was involved in a negotiation in Washington, D.C. where a man took his young wife hostage. He was threatening to kill her because she was spending all of his retirement monies. His first wife passed away. He recently married a younger woman. He earned many incentive awards for his work in the intelligence community during World War II and had accumulated many monetary awards and some royalties for his service and writings. He had just learned of her extravagance and self-indulgence at his expense and was very upset. It was clear to me that the man was proud of his preretirement accomplishments, as well he should have been. I had read of his work and was very impressed. Now, he was in a crisis, and I was faced with helping negotiate the safety, if not the life, of one of my boyhood heroes.

Through the secondary negotiator, I passed notes to the primary stressing some of the ALS listed above. Because of the stress level, silence worked well. The man had a tale to tell, so "we" encouraged him to tell us his story. This involved his work in the intelligence community during World War II. I am a history buff whose father and many uncles fought in that war. As an elementary school student, I followed the war in both theatres because my dad and some uncles were in Europe, and two of my uncles were marines in the Pacific. All this is by way of saying that I was able to provide the primary with notes of minimal encouragers that bore on the discussions of the application of intelligence in various battles. By that I mean the negotiator was able to say something like, "Wow, my uncle was with the First Marines on the Canal, so I bet they used the stuff you developed, or I had an uncle in the Navy at the Battle of Midway and I know they used what you created to figure out what the Japanese were trying to do." In addition, the subject discussed things he did that were still classified. I was able to pass notes suggesting he say things like, "I heard about that, but I think it is still classified." These are some examples of "expanded" minimal encouragers. The primary also used silence very well. However, on more than one occasion, we had to cover his mouth so he would remain quiet while the subject vented on his deeds and the spending spree of his young wife.

Eventually, the subject agreed to come out. Come out. Not surrender. His condition was that he be allowed to talk with the primary about World War II. The subject said, "I have given many lectures at universities on my work during the war. No one in any of those audiences understood what I did and how I did it as well as Officer Jones. He is brilliant." Well, "Jones" is a great guy and a good negotiator. I am not so sure about brilliant. As I recall, "Jones" was born in 1961. My job was to give him a quick synopsis of World War II so he could carry on an intelligent conversation with the hero. According to "Jones," the postincident discussion went well because he just used the same ALS he perfected during the negotiations.

The point of all this is quite simple. It works when we keep our mouth shut and let the emotionally driven subject do the talking. This is not a control issue. It is just a commonsense approach to encourage the emotional person to talk about his perceptions, stress, and situation. In the course of his talking, we gather intelligence on his I.Q., his perception of reality, his dedication, and many other clues that will help us ensure a peaceful conclusion. We listen for the "hooks" and "hot buttons."

Hooks

A hook is a topic or person we can use to extract the subject from this crisis. Several are identified in the following chapters.

Hot Buttons

Hot buttons are the opposite. They are topics and persons we want to avoid discussing. Like hooks, several are identified in the following chapters. Listening and learning will take longer than telling him what to do. However, we must use time to defuse the siege and bring everyone out alive. As negotiators, we must operate as if we are getting paid by the hour not by the job. Remember, a surgeon waits for the anesthetic to take effect before making an incision. So we, as negotiators, the tactical element and on-scene commanders, should wait for time and fatigue to take effect before we take action.

A Team Effort

There are those who may say that is we have a good negotiator, we do not need a team. Recent research has shown there are more than 166 tasks required of a negotiator during this life-saving process (Birge, 2012). All of these tasks and responsibilities induce stress. We have all been in difficult situations when, after it was over, we remember things we should have said or done. We did not say or do them earlier, we forgot, we could not focus, because of stress. The negotiation team can very effectively reduce this situational stress.

A Quick Example from Boot Camp

Speaking of stress, I recall as a young marine in "Boot Camp" being so stressed that I could not remember my name. I was walking from the wash rack back to the barracks to get my cleaning bucket. As I walked, actually marched and counted cadence to myself, I was thinking how great it was to have Sunday afternoon off. I had not seen our senior Drill Instructor (DI). I assumed and thanked God that he was not around. I was very relieved. Then, suddenly he, my DI, Sergeant Walker, a giant of a man at 5'7", appeared before me. I stopped. Actually, I froze. He looked me in the eye and asked me my name. Do not try to introduce logic and wonder how a man of 5'7" can look a person of 6′1″ in the eye. Trust me, he did. He spoke saying, "What's your name son?" I drew a blank. He asked me again. Still blank. Mind you, my name was on my cap, on my shirt, my trousers, my belt, my skivvies, socks, shoes, and every item I was issued. It was not between my ears. I was sweating bullets trying to remember my name. He asked me again. I knew I had to say something or induce the wrath of my DI. I remembered I was going to the barracks to get my bucket. I responded, "My name is on my bucket and my bucket's in the barracks." He immediately did a right face, marched off, and called over his shoulder, "Carry on."

DIs do not laugh. Perhaps he did. I entered our barracks and removed my cover, and there was my name on the bill. I arrived at my rack. There on my towel was my name. I opened my wall locker and there was my bucket with my name. I briefly thought about chasing after Sergeant Walked to tell him I now knew my name, but I thought better of it. My stress level lowered and logic prevailed.

My point is simple. Under stress many of us do not function as well psychologically as we should. When stressed physically, our adrenalin level increases and provides extra energy. Unfortunately, our brain does not have such an emergency backup system. It does not function as well under stress as our bodies. The negotiating team helps reduce stress and thus introduces some logic, intelligence, and professionalism to this life-saving process. They make us, the negotiator, look good, and the courts are pleased when we do our job correctly.

All too many people believe that a good negotiator is a good talker. I hope I have shed some light on the fact that listening, active listening, is more important than talking. Second, and some might say first, it is important that negotiators work as part of a crisis response team that includes elements of command, intelligence, tactical, and negotiations. Each of these elements is a team effort. That's right, a team effort. Within each element there is a team leader like the Incident Commander, Intelligence Chief, Tactical Commander, and Negotiations Team Leader. I will focus on the negotiations team.

Within the negotiations team, there are several roles. Described **in brief**, they are:

Team Leader: His or her job is administrative. Among other things, he or she selects personnel, arranges for training, coordinates with other elements, and commands the negotiations response.

Primary Negotiator: The primary negotiator is the person who deals directly with the subject. He or she is the voice of the team and represents the on-scene commander.

Secondary Negotiator: This person is often called the coach. That is one of his or her jobs. He or she is the on-site right arm of the negotiator. He or she assists in listening and screens written suggestions from others. He or she also monitors the primary and recommends a break for or a change in the primary.

Intelligence: The leader of this team should be an experienced negotiator because she or he has a better sense of the type of information those actually negotiating need and can use. This unit is busy gathering information from many sources. It would be best for this unit to be staffed by trained negotiators because they appreciate and understand the need for certain types of information. However, properly led by an experienced and trained negotiator, they can sort out information and intelligently decide what should be forwarded to the secondary for consideration by the primary. These people are busy asking questions of sources and setting leads for officers and investigators in the field.

Think Tank: This group is "The Brains of the Outfit." They listen to the recordings of negotiations over and over again. They listen for and identify hooks, hot buttons, and intelligence needs. Again, a hook is something we can use to get him out, and a hot button is a topic we try to avoid.

Messenger: This person or persons physically carry communications like Negotiation Positions Papers to command for their information and signature.

Guard: This person stands at the door to keep unauthorized people out of the negotiations area.

Chronographer: This person or persons keeps a log of events and often mans the "Situation Board."

Radio Operator: This technician ensures the equipment operates efficiently and effectively.

Tactical Liaison: This member of the tactical team provides immediate approval for or rejection of a change in the tactical plan for its various functions like delivery, release of people, and surrender.

Mental Health Consultant: This person helps just about everyone on the crisis response team. They assist in developing strategy for the negotiator, contact other mental health professionals for intelligence on the subject, and assist all in dealing with the stress of the siege.

Interpreters: This term is plural for a good reason. It is best to have at least two on-scene interpreters so they can agree on the proper translation of the meaning and intent of words and phrases. By way of example, I was in one siege where the negotiator was telling a Spanish-speaking subject about the surrender phase. He told him to leave his weapon inside. Once he exited, he should stop three steps from the door and kneel down. Then the tactical team would cuff him. This communication created a problem because the negotiator used a slang term for "handcuff him." One negotiator translated this as assault. Fortunately, the other understood the slang and made the correction before it was passed on to the subject. In addition, while one is listening to the subject, the other can give the negotiator a quick summary of what is being said while waiting for the subject to finish and the full report from the other interpreter.

Again, what I have written above is a brief listing of the many team responsibilities. Most books on negotiations devote at least one chapter to the negotiating team. This is a team effort. One on one isn't fair or smart. There is too much to do and too much at stake for one person to take on all these responsibilities. Remember, it is our job to save lives not save time or money.

Negotiation Position Papers (NPP)

From time to time, this team should communicate the status, plans for, and progress of this process to command. It is a tool to help keep command in the loop and is discussed in depth in the referenced article (Dalfonzo & Romano, 2003). In all honesty, one good reason to use them is to verify in a written form the recommendations and rationale of this process to command. This is also known as covering your backside (CYA). I learned that lesson in graduate school. When working in a bureaucracy, put your ideas in writing and pass them up the chain. This forces the powers that be to respond.

I used this for the first time when I was teaching a group of Indian negotiators. India is known for its levels of and experience with bureaucracy. They introduced a new twist in this process. In addition to delivering periodic position papers, they printed two copies. One was given to command, and the other was signed by command and re-tained by the negotiating team. I realize that command staff in our great nation would never deny the receipt of a communication warn-ing them of a dangerous consequence of their decision. However, it was apparent to me that this had occurred in India. So for what it is worth, I have passed it along.

Basically a Negotiation Position Paper is a status report that in-cludes recommendations. To save time and space, I have included a sample in Chapter 4. As a good frame of reference, I recommend the reader take the time to read the brief but succinct LEB article (Dal-fonzo & Romano, 2003).

Demands

When dealing with people, one cannot overgeneralize. That said, we typically hear two types of demands. Psychologists call them "expressive" and "instrumental." **Expressive demands** are most com-mon among subjects who have a mental problem. In addition, those who some call terrorists fall into this category, as do some suicidal sub-jects. They have a story to tell. They want to express their views, their innocence, their grief, their problems, etc. Once this is accomplished, most of them are prepared to come out. Criminals commonly make **instrumental demands**. They want something for themselves. Crimi-nals, who I discuss in the next chapter, are The Bad hostage takers. They most commonly have an Antisocial Personality Disorder. For them, life is "All about me." They are more than selfish or self-cen-tered. Their entire life focuses on "What's in this for me." Therefore, as hostage takers, they typically want something like money and es-cape.

Surrender Synonyms

In my experience, many, if not most, subjects, are reluctant to admit defeat. The word *surrender* strongly suggests failure or defeat. Therefore, some synonyms or softer statements may help. The follow-ing come to mind: pack your chute, fold your tent, come out and tell your story, walk out, walk away, walk out like a man, walk into the future, exit with honor, exit with dignity, throw in the towel, and return to fight another day.

References

Birge, R. (2012). Personal conversation, January 16, 2012.

Dalfonzo, V. A., & Romano, S. J. (2003, October). "Negotiation Position Papers: A Tool for Crisis Negotiators," *FBI Law Enforcement Bulletin,* pp. 27–29.

Noesner, G. (2010). *Stalling for time.* New York: Random House.

Santayana, G. (1905) In J. Bartlett (1960) *Book of familiar quotations.* Little Brown, Boston,

Strentz, T. (2005). *Psychological aspects of crisis negotiations.* Boca Raton, FL: CRC Press.

Strentz, T. (2012). Psychological aspects of crisis negotiations (2nd ed.). Boca Raton, FL: CRC Press.

Chapter 2

THE BAD (ALSO KNOWN AS CRIMINAL SUBJECTS)

Because I have a background in mental health, I find it easier to deal with people when I have some sense of their perception of reality. That is to say, are they normal or not? In the case of many criminals, particularly the repeat offenders, we are usually dealing with a person who has an antisocial personality disorder (ASP). I like the acronym ASP because it reminds me of the snake that killed Cleopatra. The best text I have read that describes this person is titled *Without Conscience: The Disturbing World of the Psychopaths Among Us* by Dr. Robert D. Hare (Hare, 1993). He is a psychologist with the British Columbia Department of Corrections. In that capacity, he has had many dealings with the ASP. His book title says it all. That text deals with the ASP in prison. His more recent work, *Snakes in Suits,* focuses on the ASP in the business world who are not yet in prison (Babiak & Hare, 2007).

These people, criminals, inmates, and entrepreneurs are male and female of ever race, color, and creed. They move through life leaving a broad trail of tears and empty wallets in their wake. They use and abuse others because it suits them. As Dr. Hare says so well, psychopaths are social predators who charm, manipulate, and ruthlessly plow their way through life, leaving a broad trail of broken hearts, shattered expectations, and empty wallets. They are completely lacking in conscience and feelings for others, as they selfishly take what they want and do as they please, violating social norms and expectations without the slightest sense of guilt or regret (Hare, 1993). As Dr. Audrey Honing of the Los Angeles Sheriff's Department says so well, their motto is, "It's all about me." As an example, think of the heartless child molester or rapist whose only interest in people is the gratification they can provide. As one ASP who had killed dozens of people told me, "People are born to die. We all die sooner or later. All I did was speed up the inevitable."

EEK

Like Doctors Honing and Hare, I have had my share of encounters with this type of person. My most memorable was during part of my master's degree program. I did a fall semester internship at The Atascadero State Hospital for the Sexual Psychopath (ASH) on the Central California coast. This was and remains a secure facility. We had guards, walls, fences, sally-ports, barbed wire and many security cameras. Most hospitals are not so equipped. I had several groups and some individual patients.

All of the patients there were called mister. This applied to Mr. Edward Ethan Kelley (EEK) who at that time was sixteen and a member of my adolescent group. He decided to play the role of assistant therapist. This decision was his not mine. Prior to our first meeting, I read the files on each of my patients. I was struck by EEK's cold-blooded killing at age 15 of his grandparents. I was also curious about his I.Q. Unlike other patients' folders, the I.Q. entry on his intake workup form was blank.

During our first session each patient sat and introduced himself as he spoke briefly of his offense. When it was his turn, EEK stood up and walked around the room. By standing he emphasized his height, well over six feet. By walking he exercised dominance and control over the group. In the course of his presentation, he said they were all there to gain insight into their sexual proclivities. I had to look that up. In addition, he said he was mortified by the attempts of some patients to soft peddle their crimes. I knew the term *mortified,* however, not too many 15-year-olds do. He used the term *female* to refer to his mother whom he hated, then said "Excuse my euphemism." He used other multisyllable words as he expressed his gratitude for being granted membership in this select group led by such a gifted therapist. (And so the con job began.)

After this session, I met with my mentor, Dr. Anderson, who was a psychiatrist. In the course of discussing my adolescent group, I asked about the missing I.Q. score for EEK. Dr. Anderson said it was left blank because we did not know how smart he was. I questioned this. He said that no matter what I.Q. test EEK took, he scored beyond its limits. The testing battery included the Stanford-Binet. Bottom line, he was so smart that no test could accurately identify and record his level of intelligence. There was not enough space on the form to write "Damn Smart."

As the semester progressed, he met me each morning at the front door just past the sally-port. He walked me to my office as he described the progress he made with "our" adolescent group thanks to my brilliant insight. (In my many years, he is the only person to ever refer to me as brilliant. I have a learning disability known as dyslexia. I learned early in life that I was not brilliant.) Our group met with me each MWF. He called them together each Tuesday, Thursday, and Saturday to follow up. Again, this was his idea, not mine. Dr. Anderson suggested I let his efforts run their course. I later learned what he meant.

I shared my "office" with three other graduate students. EEK has his own office and his own coffee pot. If you ever worked in an institution, you know that having your own coffee pot is a status symbol. As a patient, he was on the ASH intake staff. He was responsible for the administration of various tests and helping new patients adjust to the hospital. He was disarmingly friendly and engaging to all he met at ASH and years later at the California Department of Corrections facility in Vacaville. In this regard, the U.S. Postal Inspectors have a saying about con artists: "If it sounds too good to be true, it probably isn't." I have found that expression very helpful in the early identification of the ASP. In my experience, they come on strong early in a relationship and tend to "oversell" themselves.

As part of my studies, I contacted family members of my patients. I met two of EEK's older sisters who were married to police officers. As I recall, one was actually a deputy or a dispatcher. The point is they were law-abiding citizens.

They told many stories of their childhood with EEK. One included them walking home with him after his first day of kindergarten. They were kidding him about his infatuation with his teacher. One said to him, "I bet you would like to kiss her." His response at age five was, "Yes. But I would have to kill her first." At age five, I wanted to be a G-man, and he was contemplating homicide. Another story was about the game he called "Gas Chamber." They would tie him to a chair and then stand there and make hissing sounds while he writhed and finally fell over "dead."

The point of this is that EEK was "off the rails" early in life. There are other stories of dragging a Montana police officer along the road, who reached into his car to remove the ignition key, for several miles by rolling up the window and catching his upper torso in the partially closed window. As I recall, he was eleven at the time. However, he was tall for his age. On another occasion, he attempted to bludgeon his stepfather to death after "accidentally" shooting him while they were hunting.

While spending the summer with his mother's parents in California, he came to the attention of the authorities. They lived in the mountains. While there, he shot and killed his grandparents because he wondered what it would feel like to kill someone. So he exercised his intellectual curiosity and shot both of them several times. He then calmly called his mother and told her not to worry about buying an anniversary present for her parents because he had just killed them. He said that with as much emotion as a normal person would recount a routine walk in the park. Because of his age and demeanor, the courts remanded him to the care and custody of the California Department of Mental Health while a "hold" was in place by the California Department of Corrections.

One morning toward the end of that fall semester, EEK did not meet me at the front door. Frankly, I was relieved. That day he said nothing in our group. I learned from other patients that EEK had cancelled their Tuesday, Thursday and Saturday sessions. His excuse was that he was just too busy at intake. I discussed this change in behavior with Dr. Anderson. He smiled and passed me the journal he had been keeping on our sessions. He told me to turn back to our early sessions in September and look for mention of EEK. There it was in black and white. After one of my descriptions of his gregarious nature and willingness to help was the notation, "We shall see how long this lasts." I asked Dr. Anderson what he meant. He said that he suspected from the start that EEK was using me. When EEK learned I would be leaving at the end of the fall semester in January, he dropped me like a bad habit. His annual review was in March when I would be back on campus in far away Fresno and could not do him any good.

After spending several years at ASH, he was remanded to the Adult Authority with a few ASH recommendations. The first was for continued custody, evaluation, institutionalization, and treatment. The second was that, should he ever be considered for parole, he should not be paroled to the care and custody of his mother. It was clear that he hated her, and she was not particularly fond of him. Evidence of this negative relationship was her fear that as a young boy he would sexually assault his sisters. To prevent this, his bedroom was in the basement of their home. Further, the door from the basement to the main living area was locked each night.

For what it is worth, I spent my early years in Chicago. We had a basement. I never went down there alone after dark because I "knew" it was a dangerous and dark place where all sorts of evil dwelt. I cannot imagine being forced to sleep down there. Tragically, in their wonderful wisdom and insight, the Adult Authority paroled him to his mother, who was then on the library staff at a university in California. They live in an apartment in nearby. She constantly berated him for not being a man. She said that if he was half the man he thought he was, he would be dating one of the attractive, athletic, and academically gifted coeds at the university rather than the "white trash" he was seeing. EEK had an auto accident and collected quite a handsome settlement from a driver who ran a stop sign. He did not have to work, so he spent his days driving his "bike" and his mother's car around town. His mother's car had a university parking sticker on the bumper. He began picking up female hitch hikers and engaging them in conversation. Remember, he was disarmingly gregarious and very charming. He learned they felt safe in his car because of the university parking sticker clearly visible on the vehicle. His passengers were always female college students heading to work, school, or home. He fantasized about killing them. This urge, according to him, was especially strong after he and his mother had an argument about his unemployment and dating "white trash."

In his video appearances, EEK tells us that he practiced his killings. He practiced keeping his victims engaged in conversation and relaxed as he drove, often via a shortcut through a remote area, to their destination. He calls this period of his life "Fifty weeks of planned killing." He was on parole for just over fifty weeks. The producers were so impressed with this term that they used it as the title for the video.

He killed almost a dozen female hitchhikers. He also killed his mother. Like his other victims, he decapitated her. Like his other victims, he used her head to orally copulate himself. To add fuel to the fire, each time a coed "went missing," his mother would lament the fact that such a lovely young girl was gone and her contribution to our society was lost. She mourned each and every one of them. Therefore, EEK was getting even with his mother yet again. He was killing, mutilating, and sexually assaulting those she cherished.

The killing of his mother was not an intelligent act. He did not plan to kill her. He lost control during an argument and slowly strangled her. His other victims had been strangers whose bodies were not found until he confessed. In a plea bargain agreement, he led officers to their burial sites in several California counties. Once he finished with his mother, he knew he had to flee. This included a sexual assault on her remains and an attempt to dispose of her vocal chords via the garbage disposal unit in their sink. He later calmly commented that even the garbage disposal could not deal with her vocal chords. He needed time to get away. He killer her on Friday evening; she would not be missed until Monday. However, she had a friend who might visit. He called her friend. On a pretext, he lured her to their apartment, where he killed and mutilated her. He fled California in his mother's car. He listened to an all news station and did not hear any mention of her death. He called the sheriff's office long distance and asked to speak to a deputy he knew who was working the coed killings. He had socialized with him at "The Court Room." It is law enforcement "hang out" near the county court house. For reasons beyond the scope of this book, the deputy told the dispatcher to stall EEK while a unit went to the apartment EEK shared with his mother. When the unit reported finding the two mutilated bodies and several skulls, the deputy kept EEK on the line, traced the call, and waited while the local police in Colorado found the pay phone he was using and arrested him.

EEK was sentenced to life in prison because he cooperated with authorities. He is now incarcerated at the California Department of Corrections Adult Reception and Guidance Center in Vacaville, California. There, like at Atascadero, he is not just an ordinary inmate. He has a public relations job. Because he is so well spoken, he has over the years been featured on several TV programs. On one, after recounting his well-rehearsed murders of female hitch hikers and urging girls not to "thumb a ride," he reflects on the untimely demise of his mother. He recounts their last argument and "How I lost it." By this he meant his emotions took control. In other words, the murder was not planned and therefore done in haste, so mistakes were made. He then regains his composure and reflects on how every homicide he committed was after "an argument with mom." Then he says, as he holds back the crocodile tears, "She is no longer with us."

Translation, show some emotion and blame her for the homicides. As discussed in more detail below, this is classic projection. So, "logically," since the person who triggered my rage and caused me to kill is "no longer with us" I am cured of this inner demon and should be released to society. Fortunately, no one at Vacaville is buying this act. I am sure he will try again. As an example of his more recent efforts, I will share the following.

When I instruct California cops and include EEK as an example of a person with an ASP, I frequently find some who have met him. The officers tell the story of taking a criminology course at U.C. Davis that includes a visit to the Adult Authority facility at nearby Vacaville. Their visit includes a facility tour. The tour is led by EEK. To ingratiate himself to them, he shows them pictures taken with visually impaired people for whom he records books on tape. He tells them he does this as a form of community service for those less fortunate than he. As you can see, he is just flowing with the milk of human kindness.

After the tour, the professor asks his students, who do not know EEK's background, their impression of him. They comment on his friendly and gregarious nature and his intelligence, and they think he is a perfect gentleman who has been incarcerated for a white-collar or other nonviolent crime. Many believe he was "famed." The professor then recounts his crimes. This is a golden learning opportunity not to be missed, and missed it is not. EEK is disarmingly charming. Like most ASPs I have met, he oversells himself. To a member of the opposite sex, ASPs sound too good to be true because they are not true. Their entire life is a lie. Remember, they consider others as tools to be used to suit themselves. You and I speak of "my wife or my husband" or "my children" with a sense of love; they use the pronoun "my" with a sense of ownership. In other words, my wife/husband and/or children are my property. This mindset is an important personality factor to keep in mind when dealing with an ASP. In addition, it is well to remember their motto: "It's all about me." In other words, to effectively communicate with ASPs you must stress how doing what you want done is really best for them.

I have included this story to set the stage for the criminal, or bad, hostage taker. They have, as Dr. Hare stated, no conscience. It is important to keep this orientation in mind when reading the following tales from the sieges managed by law enforcement and corrections teams. Remember, the criminal operates with a different mindset. People, to him or her, are objects to be used for self-gratification. With that orientation in mind, what they do as they use and abuse others makes more sense. Along the lines of trying to make sense of senseless crimes, they typically use two psychological defense mechanisms described below: rationalization and projection.

Rationalization or Rationalizing Defined

Let me begin by saying that from time to time we all rationalize. Occasional use is normal. That is to say, we excuse an action or a failure by some general justification. Some call this thought process "sour grapes." That expression refers to a person who tries to grab some grapes but cannot, so he or she moves on saying to himor herself something like, "No doubt they were bad tasting grapes. That is why no one else got them before me." So, the person feels better about a failure. Basically it is an attempt to justify or cushion the effect of falling short of a goal.

A normal use of rationalizing is to say to one's self or others after scoring below the cutoff point on a promotional exam, "I really did not want that job. I am happy where I am." Certainly there are times when this statement is true. However, when the exam is given again, the normal person who rationalized the previous low score studies harder or seeks additional help. Again, the use of rationalization gets us past the immediate pain of failure. Rationalizing becomes pathological when one **repeatedly uses it to justify illegal or immoral acts** by thinking or saying something like, "Everyone does it or everyone is going to die sooner or later. All I did was hasten the inevitable."

It Aint My Fault (Also Known to Psychologists as Projection)

A Washington, D.C. incident involved a thwarted bank robber who claimed that the quick response of the police forced him to take hostages. This case seems odd unless one understands the defense mechanism of projection. Briefly, a defense mechanism is, according to Freud, one way that the ego protects itself from harm. From time to time, we all use defense mechanisms. They help us salvage our bent ego and progress past a failure. The key phrase is "from time to time." Those who have various mental maladies use them regularly and excessively to excuse irrational or illegal behavior.

Projection Defined

The defense mechanism of projection is more pathological than rationalizing. It is seen in most personality disorders and is considered by many as the basis for paranoia. It is an extremely powerful psychological ploy that serves to enhance one's self-concept in the face of evidence to the contrary. Basically, people employing projection believe that nothing negative in their life is their fault. They place the blame/responsibility for their problems and predicaments onto others. In this process, they view the world and events in refraction. You will recall that EEK blamed his mother for his murders. This defense mechanism is so ingrained that I am convinced even a polygraph would show no deception when the ASP blames others for his actions.

Over the years, their practice of this ploy becomes more ingrained in their social interactions and therefore more effective. It works for them. They emerge as a victim. They get damn good at blaming others for their faults. It is frequently so effective that they not only convince themselves that "others" are to blame for their problems, but they put these "others" on a "guilt trip" over their role. They are masters at this manipulation.

In the negotiations process, it is important for us to recognize this defense mechanism and remember that here we have a subject who considers himself a **victim**. In law enforcement and corrections, we typically treat victims differently than we treat subjects. Here we have a subject who thinks he is a victim. So the best approach is to make the mental shift and treat him as a victim. Go with his psychological ploy to "Get into his head," gather intelligence, and develop rapport as we move him toward a peaceful solution or a mindset appropriate for a tactical intervention.

Because they become so good at blaming others, these others begin to believe they could or should have done more to help. Others who are close to them begin to believe that, because of their role in these people's lives, they are at least partially responsible for them not achieving their potential or experiencing some or a series of failures. They begin to believe it might be their fault, or at least they had more than a minor role in creating or contributing to the adversity. Thus, they fall into the trap the ASPs have set for them and try to rectify the problem that is not their fault but for which they feel somewhat responsible. This, of course, is exactly what the projecting person, the ASP, wants and all too often achieves. People who are kind, considerate, and compassionate are especially vulnerable to this manipulation and subsequent attempt to rectify a problem that is really not their fault.

On the lighter side is the story the famous New York Yankee Catcher, Yogi Berra. After his career with the Yankees, he became the manager of another major league team, the New York Mets, and often coached his players. During one of these sessions, he was watching a new player who was having some problems fielding grounders at first base. Yogi took his glove and told him to watch and learn. Well, Yogi had similar problems and finally gave the glove back and said, "Young man, you have so fouled up first base now no one can play it properly." Of course everyone, including Yogi, laughed. The difference is that Yogi knew he was wrong in his perception. Those who regularly use this defense mechanism believe they are never at fault. It does no good to try to correct them during negotiations. Play along with their perception. Let psychologists deal with this malady later. Remember our job is to negotiate not interrogate.

This defense mechanism becomes pathological when it is used to constantly misinterpret events and in a siege and excuse illegal behavior. By way of example, many years ago, when I was in the San Antonio Division of the FBI, I encountered my first criminal use of projection. I had the weekend duty and was called out to investigate a violation of the federal train wreck statute. I was at home when the call came, and the office told me about this assignment. I was confident the Bureau recognized my great investigative and administrative ability. As I drove to the scene, I pictured fire trucks, ambulances, and all sorts of emergency vehicles that would be under my command and control. Some who know well my lack of administrative ability call this thought process delusional or delusions of grandeur. When I arrived, I saw no such vehicles nor any train or trace thereof. I called the office to verify the location. I was at the right place. I was told to locate a KATY, I think that meant Kansas and Texas Railroad, detective. I walked down to the tracks and spotted a lone adult male wearing a suit walking in my direction. I identified myself as did he. Then he said the magic words, "Damn Kids." I used my best interviewing tactic and said to him, "Damn kids?" He responded saying they had piled debris on the tracks, the train hit the stuff, and a train power or communication line was broken. This constituted a violation of that law.

Then reality kicked in. I would work, solve the case, and then turn my efforts over to the San Antonio and KATY police. I would not get any credit from the Bureau. In those days, under Hoover, getting credit was the name of the game. Long story short, I heard some kids playing. I walked up the embankment into a playground, "leaned on nine-year-olds," and identified my culprit. I went to his house and knocked on the door with my right hand as I held up my credentials in my left. His mother answered the door, saw me with my credentials, and immediately responded, "The railroad should not leave all that junk along the tracks." I think that is what the courts call a spontaneous admission. I agreed with her and called the police. A juvenile officer arrested her darling little boy and off they went to the station. The point is, her little darling was not at fault. It was KATY's fault for leaving debris along the tracks. That is projection.

Back to the Bank Robber

In the case of the bank robber, projection was his excuse for taking hostages. You must understand that the person using this excuse, this defense mechanism of projection, genuinely believes it is true. This situation involved an attempted armed robbery that was thwarted by a quick police response from units in the immediate vicinity of the bank. Their presence was obvious to the robber, who decided not to exit the building. Instead, he took several people hostage in the manager's office and used the phone in his attempt to bargain his way to freedom with his loot.

The negotiations process involved the usual search on the part of the subject for an alternative other than surrender. The fact that there was no other alternative took awhile to sink in. While you never want to underestimate your adversary, the truth is that most hostage takers are not rocket scientists. Reality typically takes time to sink in and usually involves the subject making all sorts of demands, threats and excuses. In this case, the subject finally exhausted all other alternatives and avenues of resolution.

He then said to the negotiator:

S: You know this aint my fault.

N: It ain't your fault? (This exchange went back and forth.) Then the subject said something like:

S: I was just gunna rob this bank, take the money and split. Then the cops show up and forced me to run back into the bank and take these people hostage. (Remember, the subject really believes he is a victim of circumstances beyond his control. In this case, all he wanted was to rob the bank, get the money and run . . . not get involved in a hostage siege. The subject went on to explain the logic of this course of events most of which were beyond his control and certainly not planned or his fault. The negotiator listened and made the appropriate comments.)

When he sensed that the time was right, the negotiator said something like this to the robber:

N: So where do we go from here? (Another excellent response is to play into their use of projection. Remember they firmly believe that when bad things happen to them these events are always the fault of others. An example here would be saying something like you know the longer this lasts the more likely it is that someone will be injured and then the cops and courts will blame you.)

S: You gotta tell the judge that this wasn't my fault. It was them damn cops that chased me back into the bank. I had to protect myself from them. (In his mind this whole hostage drama was the fault of the police department. He was just an innocent victim of circumstances beyond his control and wanted an assurance from the negotiator that he would explain this sequence of events to the judge.)

Ultimately, the negotiator agreed to this demand. A surrender plan had been developed by the tactical team, approved by command, and reviewed with the negotiating team. It included where he was to leave his weapon, where the hostages would be sitting, where the money was to be placed, a full description of the subject, the removal of some of his clothes, the door through which the subject was to walk, and what he was to do once out of the bank. The subject exited and was taken into custody, and off everyone went for a preliminary hearing before a U.S. magistrate.

We have learned that once we, as negotiators, make a promise to a hostage taker or suicidal person, we must keep it because chances are we, or some other negotiator, will encounter this individual again. He will remember lies as well as the good things said and done during his last siege. In this case, the negotiator said something like this to the magistrate. "Your honor it is the opinion of Mr. Jones that he was forced to take people hostage in the bank because the responding officers from the Washington, D.C., Police Department did not allow him to escape." To which the magistrate said something to Mr. Jones like "Is that your defense?" Mr. Jones agreed and was remanded to the care, custody and control of the U.S. Marshall's Service to await his trial. He was convicted of the bank robbery as well as the illegal imprisonment of his hostages.

Lessons Learned

1. One must understand the psychological defense mechanism of projection.
2. It is important for a surrender plan to be approved by command and known to the negotiating and tactical teams.
3. It is also important that the tactical team understands that no matter how hard we try to impress the subject with the importance of following the exit plan, he may not follow all of our instructions any more than your kids do everything you tell them to do.
4. For the negotiator, it is important not to unnecessarily lie to the subject. When the negotiator makes a promise, we make every effort to do what we said we would do. Again, it has been our experience that sooner or later this knucklehead will be involved

in another siege. To the negotiator, trust and the truth are as important as the sight picture is to the sniper.

5. Every effort should be made to keep any and all promises to a subject.

Was She His Mother or a "Mathar" in the Washington, D.C. Courthouse Siege?

Washington, D.C. has had its share of sieges. In the early 1970s, an incident took place in the federal courthouse basement. To set the stage, the federal courthouse, like many courts, has a holding facility for folks awaiting trial, hearings, and/or sentencing. In those days, it was in the basement. The usual procedure was for defendants to be transferred from another holding site to the courthouse in the morning to await their hearing in a secure setting. They would then be moved via an elevator from the basement to the courtroom by the U.S. Marshall's for their appearance. Typically, their time in this facility was brief and involved some contact with their attorneys to complete or sign various documents. After their appearance, most were returned to this holding site to await transport back to their more permanent cells.

One morning, this routine was dramatically disrupted. There were more than a dozen detainees in the facility, many of whom were consulting with legal secretaries, signing documents, or just waiting to be called. It remains a matter of conjecture how two defendants awaiting sentencing for a series of bank robberies were able to disarm a U.S. Marshall (USM) and take many hostages in that basement.

An alarm was sounded, and the facility was immediately secured. That was easy. The elevator was controlled by other USMs on the first floor, and the basement door was locked from the outside. The two subjects were immediately identified as were those being held hostage. The mechanics of this process were easy because everyone "downstairs" had to sign in upstairs, the detainees were on the docket ,and the USMs present were assigned to that facility. Further, their identities were verified via visual resources in the basement. The actions of all were constantly monitored via this resource throughout the siege. Unlike most sieges, we had "eyes on" from start to finish, and a tactical response was immediately and eminently available.

The telephone used to contact the facility from the court was an "in house" system–there was no TV or windows. All this is by way of saying that, given the structure of the site and the immediate availability of many law enforcement officers in the court, the response was quick and efficient. Containment was not a problem nor was manpower. Among the officers and FBI agents in court for various hearings were several negotiators as well as tactical team members. This allowed for an almost immediate beginning of a dialogue from a position of strength while a more organized response was initiated. This immediate contact provided the authorities with verbal containment and allowed for the flow of intelligence and the productive use of time.

Of course, there were jurisdictional issues. The hostage takers were the responsibility of the USM. It was a federal courthouse. However, it was located in the city of Washington, D.C. Further, this was the first such siege in this structure. These issues were resolved and a professional response was quickly in place and worked well throughout the siege.

Washington, D.C., like every American city, has in place Memos of Understanding (MOUs). Simply stated, an MOU is a document agreed to in advance of a crisis by the law enforcement, fire department, and other typical responders that sets forth responsibilities and resources for their response. This document helps bring some order to what could be a chaotic crisis response. By way of additional background, the city of Washington, D.C., has more than a dozen uniformed law enforcement agencies in addition to the Washington, D.C., Police Department. To name a few, there are the White House Police, Capitol Hill Police, those who guard the embassies, others in the Library of Congress, and the Transit Police, and each university has its officers as does the U.S. Park Police. Add to this the U.S. Marshalls, the Secret Service, the Bureau of Alcohol and Tobacco and Firearms, military police, and, of course, the FBI, just to name a few. As you might guess, law enforcement and other crisis response agencies in our nation's capital have dozens of MOUs that are regularly tested, used during training, and all too often needed to calm a crisis. On 9/11, these MOUs were credited with limiting the damage to and deaths in the Pentagon.

In addition, plans must be in place and resources identified to staff additional shifts of tactical officers, negotiators, command, and all other responders. Typically, the responders work schedules that allow coverage by two shifts each day. This reduces the congestion and confusion that always follow when three shifts are used. We learned this lesson years ago.

This setting involved two armed hostage takers, both felons with priors, who had many demands. They wanted immediate freedom, a large amount of money, transportation, and on and on. Their hostages included law enforcement personnel, civilian employees, secretaries, and others awaiting a court appearance. They were a mixed bag of folks. The negotiators listened, recorded the demands, and went to work to ensure a safe resolution as they patiently and peacefully placated the two felons.

The command post was busy organizing the response, coordinating resources, and lining up additional shifts. The names of those in the basement were readily available. However, information on their medical and mental status was not. So an immediate concern was the need for information on those being held that could be vital to their survival. This included medical concerns like a need for timely medication, its location, dosage and the name of the prescribing physician; and physical problems like heart conditions, seizures ,or other issues. In addition, information on anyone among the hostages who had a concealed weapons permit or might be carrying a weapon was vital. Granted, most people who enter a court building pass through a metal detection device. However, managers of a siege must err on the side of caution and conduct hundreds of checks on the hostages. This information-gathering effort also involves phone calls to and police presence at places of employment and the homes of the hostages. Those related to the hostages were brought "on scene" for additional debriefings and were periodically updated on the progress of this process. In the field, some officers and agents were checking with family members to learn of any "issues" that might become a factor, like a pregnant or claustrophobic hostage. Obviously this involves many jurisdictions in the immediate area and, at times, like the Branch Dividian Siege in Waco, Texas, resources in other states and folks in foreign countries. In addition, and on site, family and friends of all the defendants in the basement were identified, debriefed, and moved to a separate location. Of particular interest were those known or related to the two subjects.

As you can see, law enforcement staff and other resource requirements to effectively run and manage a siege can be enormous. In addition, as a prolonged siege moves from shift to shift, the cost also increases. In addition, a **"Think Tank"** was organized. This resource is necessary to help plan negotiations strategy. Intelligence gathered in the field from hundreds of sources is funneled through this resource. Typically other negotiators work here along with mental and physical health professionals. The use of others depends on the siege site. For instance, someone with blue prints and knowledge of the structure could be included, as could engineers, and people from the utility company, fire department, and telephone company. The listing of possible resources in the Think Tank is limited only by the imagination of those involved and the needs of the on-scene commander. By way of example, some cities automatically assign someone from the District Attorney's office to this resource. In prison sieges, a representative from the office of the governor is typically on board.

In this case, the focus was on the two subjects. There were no special problems among those being held. The two sat and negotiated from a desk that was some distance from their hostages, who sat in open cells closer to the elevator, which was at the other end of the basement.

At one point the command staff decided to use relatives of the hostage takers to convince them to surrender. For reasons unclear to just about everyone, the mother of one of them, whom I will call Ted, seemed like a good place to start. Without checking with the negotiators or learning anything about her or her relationship with Ted, an officer brought her to the negotiations desk and said to the negotiators, "The on-scene commander wants her to talk to Ted." We all have mothers. They are such loving people that we celebrate their love, dedication, and care for us with a special day in May. With that stereotype in mind, she was given the phone. The phone was passed with the naive expectation of a motherly plea for surrender. Instead she said, "Ted don't quit. The whole family is proud of you." The phone was immediately wrestled from her before any additional motherly advice was given. We learned, among other things, that there are mothers and then there are "mathars."

Somehow the negotiators and the process of negotiations survived this outburst of motherly advice. Fortunately, Ted was not that fond of his mother. Negotiators have a distinct advantage over our tactical element. We can apologize for an error. Once they pull the trigger, the bullet is gone, and the damage is done.

As the negotiations process continued, it was learned that the hostages were sneaking out via the elevator. It seems the subjects did not search the USM. One of them had a key to the elevator. Fortunately, the elevator was well-lubricated as were the doors because not a sound was made by their use. Once all the hostages were safe, the subjects were told they were alone. It was strongly suggested that an immediate surrender was in their best interest. Ted and his associate were tired, not suicidal, and smart enough to recognize that further intransigence would not be advisable. They followed the surrender plan that the tactical team had written for the negotiators earlier in the siege.

Lessons Learned

1. The continued use of a crisis response team rather than just one negotiator is important.
2. The importance of using time to our advantage while encouraging the subjects tell their story comes up again and again (Noesner, 2010).
3. Certainly the issue of using a third-party intermediary (TPI), in this case the mother, came under close scrutiny after this case. Guidelines for the use of a TPI were developed.
4. Along those lines, the interviewing and isolation of relatives of all involved was seen as an asset to the managers of this crisis.
5. The formation and use of a Think Tank to gather intelligence and make recommendations to the negotiations team is vital.

Downs v. US and Our Legal History

This case was mentioned earlier. It is by far the most significant case in this history of hostage/crisis negotiations in the United States and, by extension, the world. Like so many other sieges, Attica, Munich, Ruby Ridge, and Waco, we tend to learn our lessons the hard way. This is called the Pearl Harbor syndrome. All too often, and many times in spite of advance warnings, we do not change our thinking or tactics until we have a disaster. This phenomenon is seen in every sector of human life. Because of the impact of "Downs," it is well worth a longer discussion. Many mistakes were made. The good news is that we learned from them and adjusted our tactics and thinking. In this case, the ruling of the court, the lessons learned and the precedent set forty years ago for this dynamic process remain in effect today.

October 2011 was the 40th anniversary of a pivotal event in hostage/crisis negotiations. It is the infamous hijacking of a charter flight from Nashville, Tennessee, to Jacksonville, Florida, that was commandeered by two hijackers, George Giffe, Jr. and Bobby Wayne Wallace. This event left the pilot Brent Downs and the estranged wife, Susan Giffe, murdered and her jilted husband, George Giffe, Jr., dead by suicide. Two people survived. They were the co-pilot Randal Crump and Wallace. The hijacked aircraft was a Turbo Hawk Commander 681. Two armed hijackers in Nashville commandeered the plane. The lead hijacker George Giffe had arranged for the flight the previous morning, saying he was a psychiatrist who would be taking a patient to Atlanta for treatment. He paid for the charter in advance and left their bags at the airport for a 0200 departure.

Giffe and his associate, Bobby Wayne Wallace, then abducted Susan Giffe as she left work, held her until dark, and then drove to the airport. When they arrived, the chartered aircraft was ready to go with two pilots on board and a ground crew who had loaded their baggage. Susan Giffe began to protest. George Giffe reminded everyone that he was her psychiatrist. When the pilot asked for some medical identification, Giffe produced a Walther PPK automatic pistol and said the loaded bags contained explosives. They boarded the plane. After they left the ground crew alerted the authorities.

Once airborne, Giffe told the pilot he wanted to fly to the Bahamas. The pilot said he did not have charts, a flight plan, or enough fuel for that destination. The closest airport to the Bahamas from their location was Jacksonville, Florida. The pilot advised air traffic control of the change in destinations from Atlanta to Jacksonville and filed a new flight plan. The FAA notified the FBI, whose agents responded to the Jacksonville airport as well as other airports en route and around Jacksonville.

The commandeered aircraft landed in Jacksonville at 0508 with about seventeen minutes of fuel remaining. Ground control directed them to the Air Kamen hanger, where they stopped at 0513. The pilot requested fuel, charts, and clearance for the Bahamas. The aircraft was surrounded by FBI agents, and at 0514, the Assistant Special Agent in Charge (ASAC) J. J. O'Connor, the on-scene commander, initiated face-to-face negotiations. He was also in charge of the tactical response that in the days before FBI SWAT teams was composed of two fire-arms instructors armed with rifles. In addition, many other agents were on-scene positioned around the aircraft. Interestingly enough, these were the same responsibilities assumed the following year at Munich by Dr. Manfried Schrieber. At 0521, ASAC O'Connor told his agents they would play a waiting game.

Time Line

0508: Landed with about seventeen minutes of fuel. Some discussion with FBI as the aircraft taxied.

0513: Arrived at Air Kamen Hanger. Many FBI agents were positioned around the aircraft.

0514: O'Connor initiated face-to-face negotiations.

0521: O'Connor announced his intent to play a waiting game.

0527: Crump and Wallace exit aircraft. It was now two minutes past the original estimate of available fuel.

0529: At four minutes past the estimate of available fuel O'Connor ordered shooting to disable engine.

0530: Giff shot the pilot, his former wife and then himself. All three died in the aircraft.

Details

The following are brief negotiations between the Pilot Brent Downs (P) and the FBI agent in the tower (T).

P: 58 November. This is the captain speaking. Were going to cut engines and we're gonna need some fuel, but I request that everyone stay away.

T: 58 November. Advise when your engines have been cut.

T: 58 November?

P: This is 58 November. Un, this gentleman has about 12.5 pounds of plastic explosives back here, and (pause) uh, I got no (pause) uh, yet to join it right now so I would please expr. Un, appreciate it if you would stay away from this airplane.

T: That's a roger, 58 November. Are your engines cut?

P: Negative.

T: Standby.

P: Where's the fuel truck?

T: 58 November?

P: 58 November. Go ahead.

T: This is the FBI. There will be no fuel. Repeat. There will be no fuel. There will be no starter. Have you cut your engines?

P: Un, look. I don't think this fellow's kiddin"- I wish you'd get the fuel truck out here.

T: 58 November. There will be no fuel. I repeat. There will be no fuel.

P: This is 58 November. You are endangering lives by doing this, and uh, we have no other choice but to go along, and uh, uh, for the sake of some lives, we have requested some fuel out here, please.

T: 58 November. What is the status of your passengers?

P: Ah, uh, well, they're O.K. if that's what you mean.

T: Are they monitoring this conversation?

P: Yes, they are.

T: Do you have three passengers aboard?

T: 58 November. What's your present fuel status on that aircraft?

P: We're down to about thirteen minutes.

T: 58 November. The decision will be no fuel for that aircraft. No starter. Run it out, any way you want it. Passengers, if you are listening–the only alternative in this aircraft is to depart the aircraft, to depart the aircraft.

Shortly after this conversation, Wallace and Crump exited the aircraft and demanded fuel. They were taken into custody, searched, and hand cuffed. They were not interviewed until much later. At his trial, Wallace maintained he was a victim not a subject. For reasons unclear to everyone except the jury, he was found not guilty.

At 0529, eight minutes into the waiting game and four minutes past the estimated time of available fuel, ASAC O'Connor ordered his two snipers to fire at the aircraft to deflate the tires and disable one of the engines. The rounds bounced off the tires. Some hit the engine. It remains unclear how many agents fired at the aircraft. However, it was a number well in excess of the two firearms instructors. Giffe responded by shooting and killing the pilot, Susan, and then himself. The aircraft was so bullet ridden that it was deemed not airworthy or repairable, and today it is in the care and custody of a local technical school that offers courses in aeronautics.

The personal history of Giffe lies beyond the scope of this text. He had an Antisocial Personality Disorder (ASP). The ASP, like EEK, is your friend as long as there is something in it for them. They are disarmingly charming and deadly as the ASP who killed Cleopatra. Remember, their theme is, "It's all about me." Since Giffe could not get his way, he shot and killed as many innocent people as he could. In my mind and experience, when we are dealing with an ASP, we should remember that we are dealing with an adult who is acting like a petulant teenager. I have witnessed this attitude in many interviews with subjects who somehow survived a shooting. In my somewhat jaded judgment, the only good thing one can say about the ASP is that for law enforcement, the court system, and corrections staff, they represent job security.

The FBI was sued by the widow of the pilot and won the initial case but lost on appeal. This was the first time the FBI was successfully sued in civil court.

Lessons Learned

1. They include the importance of letting the situation play out. In the eyes of the court, the negotiations process was working as evidenced by the deplaning of two people, there was an ongoing dialogue between the hijacker and the Bureau, and the fact that no threats were made or deadlines given by the subject. In addition, the fuel level was dropping by the minute.

2. The court said the on-scene commander made an unnecessary and a hasty decision to take tactical action when the negotiations process was making progress. This process takes time (Noesner, 2010).

3. In addition, those who instruct and have experienced a siege understood that the on-scene commander played too many roles. One cannot wear three hats during such a siege. By his own admission, this was the mistake made by the Munich on-scene commander in September 1972.

4. In addition, a siege response structure must include teams led by a trained commander. Typically these teams are tactical, negotiation, and intelligence. This requirement has been reaffirmed in *Moon v. Winfield* (1974), 388 F. Supp. 31 (N. D. Ill.) and *City of Winter Haven v. Allen* (1989), 5412 So. 2nd. 128 (Fla. App).

5. The on-scene commander, like the judge at a trial, must remain independent of the elements and make decisions based on the input of the experts. The criteria typically used by the on-scene commander to determine the effectiveness of the negotiations process lie beyond the scope of this book. It is available in texts like Goergen (2010), McMains and Mullins (2010), and Strentz (2012).

Shortly before the appeals court rendered a decision, the FBI learned that it was not likely to win this appeal. Therefore, then Director Clarence Kelley ordered the Behavioral Science Unit to develop a hostage negotiations protocol. A SWAT training program was also in the works. Both were soon followed by a course for on-scene commanders. Typically, the weak line in this triad is the on-scene commander who all too often is assigned by geography or shift availability rather than training or crisis command ability. Just as not every general is a Pershing, Patton, or Chesty Puller, not every law enforcement or corrections administrator has the requisite skills to perform as the on-scene commander during a siege.

Afghanistan or San Francisco from SeaTac

Another person with an ASP hijacked the same flight twice. During the heyday of hijackings, aircrews became quite proficient in dealing with hijackers. This proficiency was the result of an FBI, FAA, and Commercial Carrier training program. In this case, a young man, Mr. Skipp, boarded United Airlines Flight 123 at the international airport in Seattle known as SeaTac because it is located between the cities of Seattle and Tacoma, Washington.

Shortly after he was seated in coach and while the aircraft was still at the gate, he passed a note to a female flight attendant telling her he was armed and was hijacking the plane for a flight to San Francisco or Afghanistan. Interestingly enough, the first scheduled stop for this flight was San Francisco. This was the first indicator that perhaps Mr. Skipp was not a rocket scientist. The flight attendant notified the pilot, who notified ground control who notified the airport police and the FBI. The flight deck crew evacuated the plane along with the passengers in first class. The flight attendant then invited the young man into first class. He wanted to go into the cockpit. She told him it was against FAA regulations for non-airline personnel to enter the cockpit until the aircraft was airborne. She did not say no. She said not now. He comfortably situated himself in first class. She offered him a soft drink and told him she was going to get him additional refreshments from the rear galley. She suggested that he listen to ground control via the head-set on channel 1. He put on the head-set and listened. She then closed the curtains between coach and first class as she and the others in the cabin crew quietly evacuated the 727 aircraft out the rear door. As soon as the aircraft was empty and law enforcement was in position, a negotiator contacted Mr. Skipp. He was advised that he was alone on the plane. Mr. Skipp immediately searched the coach cabin and the cockpit. He verified that he was alone and demanded that the pilot be brought back to the aircraft. He communicated this by yelling.

Two-way communications were soon achieved via a "Throw Phone." He was told that the pilot refused to return, and the union contract allowed him that option. However, an attempt would be made to locate a crew of volunteers. In addition, it was going to take time to get the right charts and clearance for a flight to Afghanistan. He was asked whether he had a passport or visa for this trip. He said no. He was told that could complicate matters. However, a contact would be made with the Department of State to see what could be done. The problem was that it was late afternoon in Seattle, and the State Department in Washington, D.C. was already closed. Other complications were created by the think tank. As the negotiations process continued, Mr. Skipp became fatigued and eventually exited the plane. He was not armed. Once in custody, a positive identification was made. A background check revealed he had a long juvenile record in San Francisco that included throwing rocks at passing police cars. He was from a broken home and had many nasty encounters with the police.

Let's Do That Again

Because of his age, Mr. Skipp was remanded to a federal juvenile facility, where he remained for a few years. Some say too few years. Shortly after his release, in time for Christmas, he returned to SeaTac. He again boarded United Airlines Flight 123. This time he did not pass the flight attendant his hijacking note until the flight was airborne. Like the first note, it said that he wanted to fly to San Francisco or Afghanistan. The itinerary of the flight had not changed. The next stop was San Francisco. He was told the plane would have to land in Portland to obtain additional charts and proper clearances. The plane landed in Portland, and the negotiations process began. Unfortunately for him, his true identity was not learned until after the incident. As he spoke with the negotiator, he told him that he had a passport. When asked about his initial destination of San Francisco, he said he changed his mind. In addition, he claimed to have a bomb. Telling the negotiator you have a bomb is an excellent way to get and keep everyone's attention and dramatically increase the stress level of all involved. No connection was made to the previous hijacking because years had passed and a different team in a different city at a different airport responded.

This time he insisted the curtain between first class and coach remain open. He learned at least one lesson from his previous attempt. However, he remained out of the cockpit because once again the flight attendant told him that FAA regulations prohibited his entry. His threats escalated as he fingered his alleged bomb. The FBI negotiating team was able to buy time with concerns over a visa, getting enough fuel for such a long flight, as well as food and other items and issues.

He refused to change planes to an aircraft that could fly non-stop. He was told that this aircraft would have to make many stops and was asked about his preferences of cities en route. The problem of his alleged explosives remained, and he regularly made comments about blowing up the plane and/or leaving the scene in a flash with everyone on board. The on-scene commander made the tough decision to use a tactical maneuver. Mr. Skipp was shot and killed. He did not possess a bomb.

Once his true identity was learned, a search warrant for his residence was obtained, where no evidence of explosives were found. Further, interviews of acquaintances determine he was not known to have any knowledge of explosives. Frankly, I believe Mr. Skipp was engaged in a process known as "Suicide by Cop." He manipulated law enforcement into a situation where the on-scene commander in Portland, like the on-scene commander previously mentioned in Silver Spring, had no choice but to order a tactical intervention.

Lessons Learned

1. Do not say no. Say not now.
2. Keep him out of the cockpit, quote rules and regulations, and the union, take time, and count on the crew for help. They have been trained in "The Common Strategy." Have you?
3. Take time and use your think tank to review the negotiations in a search for a hook. In this case, no hook was identified. It remains unclear what he planned to gain from this venture.
4. As negotiators, we must remember that trying to make sense out of what a subject is saying or demanding may not be a viable alternative. People who are crazy or deranged do not always make sense.

Good Coffee Takes Time

Another situation took place in a Washington, D.C., bank that involved a trapped gunman. I have forgotten the mechanics of how he became trapped in the bank. However, given the proficiency of the Washington, D.C., Police Department and many other law enforcement agencies in our nation's capital, it is not unreasonable to suspect that once again a rapid response resulted in a sudden change in his plans.

In this case, he wanted around $70,000 in a variety of denominations. Of course, he also wanted a get-away car, or it could have been a helicopter. Be that as it may, his plan was to make everyone pay for trapping him in the bank and forcing him to take people hostage. His demands also included a cup of coffee with two spoons of sugar and some cream. His demands were sent up the chain of command by the negotiating team, and the protracted process of negotiations played out. Of course there were questions about the type of coffee. He did not want McDonalds or Hamburger Heaven coffee. Their options are basically limited to three: caffeine, decaffeinated, or a mix of the two. He wanted Starbucks coffee. To some this request might suggest he had some class. To the negotiating team, this meant many options. Starbucks has hundreds of coffee types and combinations. A menu was procured, and a long discussion followed about which type of coffee, and cream, how much sugar, and on and on. Of course the subject voiced the usual threats of having a hostage drink some first to make sure the coffee was not drugged. In addition, the Starbucks menu offers a variety of donuts, cakes, and so on. More than an hour passed before the coffee delivery could be initiated, plus additional time was necessary to implement the mechanics of a safe delivery. When the coffee arrived there was no sugar, no cream, and it was cold. The good news is that by that time, the subject was sufficiently fatigued and had come to the realization that if it took that long for coffee, at fifty cents a cup, it could take forever to meet his other demands.

The siege finally ended with the subject saying something like, "I wanted seventy thousand dollars and I began doing some figuring." Remember he was in a bank, where there are adding machines and calculators. He decided that if a fifty-cent cup of coffee took two hours, then his $70,000 would take about eight years to arrive. Do not hold me to the math. I think you get the idea that he recognized the reality of his situation. We used time to wear him down and frustrate him. As anyone who has been involved in a siege knows, most of the time laps and frustration were real and not intended. It takes time to get that much money and for the tactical team to develop, work out, and get approval and authority to safely deliver the coffee or anything else. Again, properly done, these things take time. Then there are the mechanics of a safe delivery. We have learned that in a hostage siege, unlike most crises, when properly used, time can work for us as we avoid the action imperative and let the situation play out. This requires a change of mind-set. Usually, the quicker we respond in a correctional setting or law enforcement encounter, the more likely we are to succeed. That rule is generally not true during the proper management of a hostage siege.

Lessons Learned

1. The lessons learned here include the effective, logical, and believable use of time to properly and safely meet his demand for coffee. Again, the devil is in the details.
2. Listen for the hook, as we try to figure out what he really wants, and then use it to bring the siege to a safe conclusion.
3. We can also deliver things he does not want because we acted too fast, and in the process of attempting to please him, made some mistakes.
4. Typically, the subject is searching for a nonexistent escape alternative. During the negotiations process, his adrenalin level will gradually subside, and reason will begin to replace emotion. This physiological process takes time (Noesner, 2010).
5. This has been clearly demonstrated during prison sieges like the federal facility in Atlanta where the subjects accepted on day five what was offered on day one and later in Arizona where the subjects accepted on day fifteen what was offered on day five. It took time for them to ventilate and tell the world that they were the real victims of the authorities who were the real cause of this siege.
6. As negotiators, we must remember that typically we are dealing with a subject who considers himself a victim. Obviously and logically, this is psychological projection. However, to the subject, it is reality, and it is his reality that we must address. We treat victims and family members differently than we treat criminals or convicts. Here we have a criminal or convict who considers himself the victim. Therefore, negotiators must adjust the approach to fit the mind-set with which they are dealing. This is not to say negotiators agree with them. Rather, negotiators are just trying to communicate more effectively. This procedure concept must be understood by command and tactical who may be listening to the negotiations process.

I'll Do It My Way

When I was in the FBI, we did a study to identify and examine those situations and sieges in which our tactical element shot the hostage taker. My part was the personality types of the subjects. In quick summary, most of those we shot were trying to hijack a commercial aircraft. The others were involved in bank robberies or had taken hostages to ensure their escape. None ever succeeded. All of those we shot were criminals with long records and at one time or another were diagnosed as having an ASP. I like the acronym of ASP. Again, you will recall from your high school history, or was it literature, that an ASP bit and killed Cleopatra. Just as an ASP is a deadly snake, the human ASP is a deadly predator. They are the serial killers and rapists. The earlier examples from Atascadero and Dr. Hare made this point.

Such was the case with John. That was not his real name. It was the name he gave us. Once we identified him, a discussion followed to determine whether we should confront him with what we knew or continue using the name he gave us. For reasons beyond the scope of this story, we stayed with the name he gave us (see Figure 1).

John was on parole for a series of crimes that included assaults on women when he tried to rob a bank. The bank was in a shopping center near his psychologist's office. A condition of his parole agreement was to regularly visit his psychologist. Ordering a person to participate in therapy is like ordering a person to get into shape by purchasing a gym membership. Therapy and physical exercise require involvement and work to reap the benefits. If the person with the gym membership visits the gym, smokes a cigarette or two, wanders around the spa, and then goes home, he will not physically benefit from his membership. The same holds true for therapy. One must get with the program. Typically, ASPs believe they are O.K. Other people have a problem. Because "they are O.K.," no need for therapy. So why bother?

I recall a therapy session with an ASP who maintained that his most serious problem was getting caught when he committed a crime. He wanted the therapy sessions to focus on how to avoid apprehension, not to correct a condition that was not a problem for him. His basic mind-set and that of all ASPs is that they are O.K., it is the rest of the world that is out of step. You may have heard about or read the book by Thomas A. Harris titled *I'm O.K. Your O.K.* (Harris, 1967). That

Figure 1. The subject in the bank with pistol, sunglasses, and wig.

is a healthy approach to life. The mind-set of ASPs is that they are O.K. the rest of us are not.

The FBI became involved with John when he was caught trying to rob a bank. Once again, a quick patrol response trapped the robber, and again the robber took someone hostage. In this case, he terrified one teller. There were no customers in the bank, and the other employees escaped out the back door. John was there with Juanita. The bank had many windows that John eventually covered by changing the blinds. But before he could accomplish this, the first responders did not see any customers in the bank. Further, an interview of the on-

Figure 2. Subject with hostage in the bank.

duty manager revealed that Juanita was alone in the bank. He had accounted for his other employees (see Figure 2).

A police lieutenant who was not a trained negotiator made the first contact. He was accustomed to telling people what to do, not negotiating or engaging in a give-and-take situation while he was in uniform. The negotiations went something like this:

Lt.: This is Lieutenant Cotter from the Big Town Police Department. Are you alone in there with that hostage?

John: (John told the lieutenant to do something to himself that was physically impossible.) Then added, "I want ten thousand dollars, police radios, and a fast car."

Lt.: Are you going to kill that hostage?

John: Same response.

Lt.: Look. We are trying to get some money for you. This is going to take time.

John: Just remember I am ready, willing, and able to kill this bitch.

Fortunately, a trained negotiations team and a well-positioned tactical unit were soon on scene and initiated the negotiations process versus the confrontation began by the lieutenant. John reiterated his demands for radios for all the local law enforcement agencies, money, and a car for his escape. For those not familiar with typical procedures in banks, once the silent alarm is triggered, the vault is automatically locked. Therefore, John was limited in his take to the money in each of the teller's windows. He was an experienced bank robber and knew that much more money was in the vault. En route to his therapist, he had watched the bank and knew when additional money was delivered. It was later learned that a few weeks ago, he made an excuse to change the day of his appointment to coincide with that delivery. But, that is getting ahead of the story.

Initially, all we knew was that the robber was a blond white male, about six feet tall, slender, and armed with a revolver. After about an hour or so into this process, a nearby psychologist, Dr. Getwell, called the police department. He identified himself and said his usual Thursday 9:30 a.m. patient, a parolee named Sam Smith, had not arrived. However, his car was parked out front. In addition, he was aware of the siege at the bank that he could see from his office. Dr. Getwell was very cooperative and provided the name of John's parole agent. Long story short, a positive identification was made. Between the psychologist and the parole agent, an excellent profile of Sam was developed, and a negotiations strategy was outlined.

The police reviewed their records and noticed that on the last few Thursdays at about 9:00 a.m., they received 911 calls from pay phones in and around the shopping center. This evidence suggested that Sam had done his homework. He probably timed the police response and figured he could rob the bank and get to his psychologist's office before the police arrived. According to his parole agent, such behavior was consistent with Sam's criminal history.

N: This is Joe Johnson from the FBI. Can you tell me what is happening in there?

Sam: I'll tell you what's happening. I got this broad hostage and if you don't do exactly what I tell you, I will kill her. (Sam did not realize it, but this sort of opening is typical of an ASP who believes he is in charge and wants to frighten people into immediate compliance. Of course we soon verified his personality type with his psychologist and parole agent who became part of the think tank.)

N: We don't want anyone hurt, and that includes you.

Sam: O.K. then you do exactly what I tell you and no one will be hurt.

N: Well, no one has been hurt so we are off to a good start.

Sam: I want a fast, unmarked car, radios from every agency in the area, and $100,000 in small bills in a bag in the back seat of the car. I want that car parked right next to the back door with the front door open and the motor running. You got that?

N: You are telling me you want a car, radios, and a lot of money.

Sam: That's right, and I want it now.

N: Well, it is going to take awhile to line up those radios. There are about a dozen agencies around here. The fast cars are owned by the highway patrol and they are all marked.

Sam: Well then you have a problem.

N: A problem?

Sam: That's right, a big problem, because if I don't get what I want, I am going to kill this broad, and then you are going to have to explain to her kids why mommy isn't coming home anymore.

N: Now don't do anything precipitous.

Sam: I am calculating my every move. (How many bank robbers know what precipitous means? This certainly established his level of intelligence that was consistent with the reports from the parole agent and psychologist.)

N: O.K. Our calculations tell us it is going to take time to line up all the things you want.

Sam: How much time?

N: That depends on the agencies from which you want radios, the type of vehicle you want, the availability of such a vehicle, and getting the money.

Sam: The ball is in your court. You know what I want. Get it.

N: Well, we just cannot get radios from them. Tell me the agencies from which you want radios and the type of vehicle you want. Further, when you said small bills, what denominations are you talking about? Do you want the money in bank bags, plastic bags, a box, or what? (The devil is in the details yet when you want to comply with the demands of a person, you must be clear on what he or she wants, otherwise time is wasted by delivering the wrong items. This requires clarification, and clarification takes time.)

A long conversation followed during which Sam specified what he wanted. During the discussion, a delivery of some money was made to the drive-in teller window to establish the presence and reasonable well-being of Juanita. Sam was an ASP and thus very impulsive. This time-consuming process was frustrating for him. What he thought would take a few minutes took hours. He was told and convinced that radios he did not know how to operate would not do him any good. Therefore, radios were delivered to the drive-in teller window, and he was instructed in their use. He was told in advance that the radios would only allow him to receive not transmit. After some prolonged discussion of the rational for this arrangement and how it was to his advantage, he agreed.

This siege began at around 9:30 a.m. By the time many of the details were worked out, it was well after noon. By the time the money was ready, it was well after 3:30. Now additional problems developed with traffic issues of the afternoon rush hour. Sam's plan remained that he would leave the bank in a fast car, with money, radios, and Juanita. No one was comfortable with the idea of him leaving the bank, especially in the company of Juanita. The psychologist discussed his past behavior and predicted future behavior. He said Sam had a history of violence. Sam treated people as his pawns. He had a history of violence toward women. In his opinion, letting Sam leave with Juanita was not a good idea. In the words of the psychologist, Sam saw Juanita as his ticket to freedom. He said that once he thinks he is free, she will become a liability. He said just as you initially value a theater ticket, once inside, what do you do with the stub? Well, he will discard Juanita, kill her, with as much emotion as you discard a ticket stub. In his mind, she goes from being needed for his getaway to garbage. Remember, he has no conscience. The negotiator tried to convince Sam to throw in the towel. He did not use the word *surrender*. Sam would not hear of it. His psychologist was allowed an opportunity to talk to him. He told him the FBI and police would not allow him to leave. Sam's response was, "They don't have any choice." He then hung up the phone. I will not go into the details of the shooting of Sam because they involve tactical maneuvers that are used today. Sam was shot and killed. Juanita was not physically injured. She was transferred from the bank to a position in their main office.

Lessons Learned

I was not on site during this siege. I was in the sub-basement at Quantico well under the cafeteria and in constant telephonic contact with those on scene. From a bureaucratic perspective, this became an issue over the years for those in Washington, D.C., and a few threatened souls at Quantico who viewed us as members of the Training Division, yet we were operational. This became a Training Division II issue versus a Criminal Division V assignment. (Don't hold me to those numbers.) Frankly, and in all honesty and candor, at Quantico, we lived in fear of being transferred from our rural delightful digs to the overcrowded "Metroplex" of our nation's capital. As a young marine, I learned then and later at the Welfare Department in Fresno that the further you are from headquarters, the more effectively you can do your job. Perhaps that is one of the reasons that I was never promoted. My focus, and those of others in the Training Division, was on helping the field function more effectively rather than gathering scalps of agents who where trying to do their job as best they could in spite of bureaucratic encumbrances. Isn't that a nice way of saying bureaucratic crap?

1. In this case, we learned the difference between a police lieutenant and others accustomed to telling people what to do versus a trained negotiator.
2. In addition the value of a psychologist and parole agent in the think tank was obvious.
3. Intelligence from the parole agent provided a review of the subject's criminal history of using, abusing, and killing women that assisted all of us. Sam's repeated threats to "Kill the girl, broad, or bitch," rather than refer to her by name, were bad signs. In his mind, she, like other women in his life, was an **object**, not a person. The analogy from his psychologist kept ringing in our ears. She was a ticket soon to become a ticket stub.
4. The negotiator used time to make every reasonable effort to convince Sam to fold his tent. He was reminded over and over again that coming into custody was an option. Sam said that anything short of his leaving the scene was an option. I guess he did leave the scene but not as he intended. This repetitive listing of some sort of surrender is crucial because too many hostage takers are not rocket scientists and must, according to the courts, be told that throwing in the towel is an option. Apparently Sam as an impulsive ASP believed he was smarter than the authorities and could make good his getaway in a fast car with lots of money and a "broad" as his shield.

The Infamous Stockholm Bank Robbery

To best understand the behavior of **some** hostages during a siege, a quick review of the attempted robbery of the Sveriges Kreditbank in downtown Stockholm, Sweden, at Normalmstorg is in order. This case is included because a gregarious and seductive ASP was and remains the hostage taker most likely to seduce his hostages into believing that he is protecting them from the police. The Stockholm victims in their post-incident discussions voiced this mind-set with their prime minister, Mr. Olaf Palme. Sweden is a small country, and folks have more access to public officials than those of us in more heavily populated nations.

To set the stage, this hostage siege gained long-lasting national and international notoriety primarily because over the almost six-day siege, the electronic media exploited the tears of the victims, the police actions, the opinions of law enforcement, and the solutions offered by too many politicians along with the sequence of events. Even the public school system got into the act with children drawing pictures of the siege and suggesting solutions. As I recall, school psychologists thought this was a good way for them to express their concerns and fears. Further, the bank is located between a heavily used commuter ferry and trolley lines and is adjacent to a road used by hundreds, if not thousands, of Swedes in their daily commute to work from the suburbs to downtown Stockholm (see Figures 3 and 4).

In addition, it became a political issue because it occurred during the campaigning for their national elections. Each candidate had his or

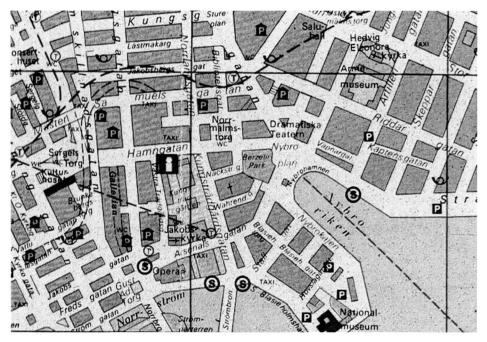

Figure 3. The routes of transport to downtown Stockholm that pass through the park in front of the bank.

Figure 4. The front of the bank. Note the apartments above the bank.

her separate siege solution that fueled the national debate. In the United States, we would say it became a media and political circus.

The Facts

At 10:15 a.m. on Thursday, August 23, 1973, the chatter of a submachine gun destroyed the quiet early and daily routine of the Sveriges Kreditbank in downtown Stockholm, Sweden. As clouds of plaster and glass settled around the 60 stunned occupants, a heavily armed, lone gunman called out in English, "The party has just begun." The "party" was to continue for 131 hours (that comes to five and one-half days) (see Figures 5 and 6). It permanently affected the lives of four young hostages and gave birth to a psychological phenomenon subsequently called the Stockholm syndrome. His choice of English is interesting because he was a Swedish former felon on parole. However, in those days, many draft-dodging Americans found their way to Sweden. I suspect this felon, Jan-Erik Olsson, was attempting to confuse the police and not divulge his true identity.

Figure 5. Here are some of the items brought into the bank. Note the passport.

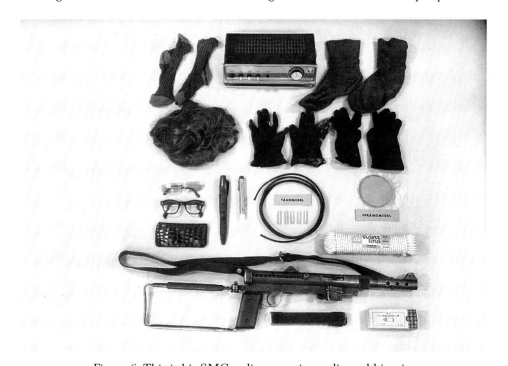

Figure 6. This is his SMG police scanning radio and his wig.

You may find it difficult to believe that a Swedish felon would speak more than one language. That is certainly true in the United States, where most felons have difficulty with English. However, in Europe, most people speak more than one language. I recall going to a locksmith in Stockholm for an extra key. I walked into his shop, and I think he said something in Swedish. I said good morning in English, and he switched to English. Granted he sounded like Tim Conway who played a Norwegian on the Carole Burnett show, but he certainly spoke English.

Back to the siege, during the 131 hours that included hours from 10:15 a.m. on August 23 until 9:00 p.m. on August 28, four employees of the Sveriges Kreditbank were held hostage in the vault under the main level of the bank (see Figure 7). It had previously served as a bomb shelter. The customers were immediately released and ran from the bank. The hostages were Elisabeth, age 21, an employee of 14 months working as a cashier in foreign exchange; Kristin, age 23, a bank stenographer in the loan department; Brigitta, age 31, a loan officer at the bank; and Sven, age 25, a new employee, today employed by the bank in a different location.

A 32-year-old previously convicted thief, burglar, and prison escapee named Jan-Erik Olsson held them hostage. His extensive criminal history strongly suggests that he was an ASP. Their jail was an 11 x 47 foot, carpeted basement bank vault that they came to share with another convicted criminal, repeat offender, and former cell mate of Olsson, Clark Olofsson, age 26 (see Figure 8). Olofsson joined the group only after Olsson demanded his release from Norrkoping Penitentiary. It is believed by some that the siege was the idea of Clark Olofsson because he was about to be transferred to another prison from which the possibility of parole or escape was minimal. Normally the government would not release an inmate. However, they saw this as moving him from one place of custody to another place of closer custody. In fact, his movement to the vault placed him in a more secured environment than the prison. The vault was also a shelter stocked with food, water, bedding, and other provisions. Therefore, negotiations for such items were never an issue. However, the vault did not have a toilet. Thus, the six adults were not very comfortable. In addition, the psychological stress of captivity initiated menstrual cycles.

Figure 7. Three hostages and one subject in the vault.

Over a period of five and a half days negotiations conducted were with both subjects and with the hostages. The hostages continued to plead the case for the subjects who, in their view, were protecting them from the police. The hostages said they would take out personal loans to pay the robbers the money they were demanding if the police

Figure 8. The vault after the siege.

would let them go. One evening the vault door was ajar. The police saw this as an opportunity to rescue at least one of the hostages who was seated outside the door. However, as an officer descended the stairs, the hostage called out and warned the robbers of his approach. They responded with submachine gun fire. As the officer beat a hasty retreat, she went into the vault and pulled the door closed.

Later the police threatened to inject knockout gas into the locked vault. The subjects responded saying they had tied their hostages and placed a noose around each of their necks with the other end secured in such a fashion that when they succumbed to the gas, they would be hanged. Intelligence revealed this was a valid threat. Further, the police feared the submachine gun fire may have struck the vault door-locking mechanism and could delay or possibly deny their entry. This could prove fatal to the hostages as they were well bound. Negotiations continued. They focused on the amount of money the subjects wanted, the form of transportation they were demanding, and their final destination, among other issues.

The police continued to delay, and thus buy time and fatigue and frustrate the subjects as they gathered intelligence. This tactic paid off when they learned the robbers had a morbid fear of tear gas. They believed that tear gas "would turn their brains to mush." When I was a teenager, I was told what would turn my brain to mush, and it was not tear gas. With this intelligence, the negotiator told the subjects that tear gas was going to be used. He told them to exit the vault immediately and unarmed. The threat went unheeded. However, the injection of the gas resulted in an immediate mass exit from the vault led by the two terrified subjects (see Figure 9). Thus, the siege ended with the capture of the subjects and release of the traumatized hostages.

Once released, and contrary to what had been expected, it was found the victims feared the police more than they feared the robbers. In a telephone call to Prime Minister Olaf Palme, one of the hostages expressed these typical feelings of the group when she said, "The robbers are protecting us from the police." The hostages puzzled publicly and in private over their feelings, "Why don't we hate the robbers?"

For weeks after this incident, and while under the care of psychiatrists, some of the hostages experienced the paradox of nightmares over the possible escape of the now jailed subjects who might escape and abduct them again. Yet they felt no hatred toward their abductors. In fact, they felt the subjects had given them their lives back and were emotionally indebted to them for their generosity. This type of fear is common in former hostages. Psychologically, they have gone from the normal attitude of bad things happen to others to an abnormally strong sense of personal vulnerability. Though this case is from Europe, similar reactions have been observed in the United States and around the world.

One explanation for this reaction goes back a few hundred years. While writing *The Prince* in 1513, Machiavelli said, "And since men, when they receive good from whence they expect evil, feel the more indebted to their benefactor" (Machiavelli, 1948). Hostages expect their captors to abuse them. Instead and on occasion, their abductors give them the impression that they care for them and are protecting them from the police. In return, the hostages feel compassion for their

Figure 9. The end of the siege.

tormentors and at times side with them against the authorities. In American history, this reaction was seen in the behavior of hostages at Harpers Ferry in 1861 and in that of the kidnapping victim Patricia Campbell Hearst about a hundred years later and in hundreds of less publicized sieges in every state and territory (Strentz, 2006, 2012).

Lessons Learned

1. The primary lesson learned from this situation was not to automatically expect the hostage to be on the side of the authorities. The goal of hostages is to survive. Their attitude is short sighted. To achieve this goal, we have seen some side with subjects and others attack them. The problem is that typically effective negotiations take time, during which hostages are under tremendous stress. Along these lines, the last thing a negotiator shall say to a hostage is "relax." If they could relax, they would be insane. A better tact is to listen. Let them tell their story of stress and fear as we assure them we are doing everything humanly possible to get the out as safely as possible as soon as possible. Assure them in advance that their release may take longer than they think and tell them of your expertise and experience in getting everyone out safely. Additional information on and about hostages is available in the second edition of *Psychological Aspects of Crisis Negotiations* (Strentz, 2012).

2. Time was used to gather intelligence on the subjects. In this case, it was their morbid fear of tear gas that provided the police with the solution.

Epilogue: The subjects were returned to prison and given longer sentences. One of them, with the assistance of a former hostage, escaped. He told her he wanted to marry her, and she believed him. After he escaped, he ditched her and fled to The Netherlands, where he married a teacher. As I recall, that marriage did not last very long. She "got wise to him" and in the process learned he was wanted in Sweden. She turned him over to the police. He was returned to Sweden and their judicial process.

Poor Me, I must steal

There was a hostage siege in Portland, Oregon, that also involved the Stockholm Syndrome but in a less public way. The jury remains out on whether this person was an ASP, a loser, or perhaps a dumb ASP. It occurred at a large hotel, and before it was over, it involved the Portland Police Bureau, the FBI, and some confused hostages.

To protect the identity of the ignorant, I will call the subject Joe. By way of background information, not known to the police at the time, Joe had worked as a gardener at the victim hotel. He cut grass for a firm that had a contract with the hotel chain. He was fired for damaging too many grass cutters by running into buildings, parked cars, fire hydrants, and other immobile objects with expensive lawn mowers. The police also did not initially know that en route to this robbery he ran out of gas, abandoned his car, and walked to the hotel. He had some knowledge of the building and knew the bookkeepers worked in a converted hotel room well off the mail lobby. He also knew that bookkeepers kept books and counted money.

He walked into the room in which they were working from the hallway and announced a robbery. He was armed with a .38 caliber revolver and brandished his weapon for all to see. Several females were in the room, including some answering the "1-800" number for the chain. Upon making his announcement, the employees went to their wallets and began removing their money. He told them he did not want their money, he wanted the money from the hotel. (This is a good start to ingratiate one's self to hostages.) His hostages began to believe that he really was not a bad person because he refused their money. He was told that the hotel money was at the front desk. All they had were receipts, debits, credit card charges, and related paper work. This took a few minutes to sink in. Their unified affirmation of this fact finally registered. They told him the cash was at the front desk. He selected one of his hostages to go there and return with his money. She left out the same hall door through which Joe had entered. I will call her C1.

Joe sat down with his remaining hostages and told them his sad story. He told them he needed money for his son's surgery and was out of work. He did not tell them about the number of jobs he had lost because of his inept handling of equipment or not coming to work. He came across to them as a poor soul who was down on his luck and needed some temporary help. He did not know about social services or the availability of medical help from the county hospital. His story went on and on as he awaited the return of his hostage with the loot from the front desk.

After awhile he began to wonder what was taking her so long. The supervisor in the room said something to the effect that perhaps she was so frightened that she just went home. The others agreed and added that she was a new employee and rather young. So a discussion was initiated to identify a replacement for and next courier who when selected had to promise to return with the money as soon as possible. One was identified. She left, and he continued to tell the remaining hostages his sad story.

When courier number two (C2) arrived at the front desk, she found C1 conversing with the on-duty manager and a uniformed Portland police officer. It took a few minutes of questions and answers for the officer to figure out what was going on because C2 immediately asked C1 why she had not returned and added that she thought C1 had gone home. C1 responded saying she did not go home; she and the on-duty manager had immediately called the police. C2 then said, "Well, we were all waiting for you to bring them the money."

The use of "we" versus "them" suggests some bonding had occurred. Research has shown, as suggested in the above story from Stockholm and Machiavelli, that "When men receive good from whence they expect evil they are more indebted to their benefactor." In this case, Joe did not verbally threaten anyone, he just told them his sad story. In so doing, he gained their sympathy. Of course, demanding money from the hotel rather than from them also helped his cause and image.

No doubt the officer listened to this exchange and others to include the manager created some sense of disbelief. After C1 and C2 finished their initial exchange, the officer stopped asking questions. He was able to verify that there was a robbery in progress to include a hostage siege. He called for backup and a negotiator. It took awhile for other units to arrive. I do not remember if there was a C3.

The negotiator was Detective Sergeant Dave Simpson. I have known Dave for many years. He attended the FBI negotiator-training course at Quantico and I believe a profiling course that I taught in Sandy, Oregon. In addition, like me, he was a former marine. By his nature and in my experience with him, Dave is a low-key person who is willing to listen to people. So, he tried to listen to Joe. He tried, but Joe was not a talker. Instead, his hostages insisted on talking for him.

This sort of behavior was well portrayed in the movie "Cadillac Man," where the hostage taker, Tim Robbins, let the phone ring and ring until one of his hostages, played by Robin Williams, answered the phone and throughout the siege negotiated for him. That is what happened in Portland. Dave spent more time on the phone with the hostages than with Joe. Try as he did, they would not get off the phone. Perhaps at some level they recognized Dave's inability to speak with, much negotiate with, a silent Joe and feared an assault by the police. Perhaps they felt sorry for Joe and just wanted to help. Perhaps they were victims of the Stockholm Syndrome.

When Joe was on the phone, he was agitated, frustrated, and upset. To calm him down, the decision was made to put some money outside the door. This became a problem because there was more than one door to that room. Dave was across the court yard looking at the sliding glass doors. The subject had entered the room and sent his hostages out the door to the corridor. So, as the discussion continued about a show of good faith from the police and the hotel by the placement of money outside the door, the tactical team was able to make the delivery. Once they had withdrawn to a position of cover, Dave told Joe the money was outside the door. There followed a discussion in the room about who would go out the door to retrieve the money. I will call her C4. Finally, C4 was identified, promised to return with the money, and walked out the door into the corridor. As she searched the corridor for the money that was outside the patio door, she was taken into custody by the police. It was the policy of the Portland Police Bureau that once a hostage exited a siege site, he or she was not allowed to return.

While this was going on, Dave and other officers were watching the patio door awaiting the exit of the arm of a hostage or someone to grab the package. Finally, a hostage got on the phone and told Dave that C4 left and had not returned. Of course Dave said that he did not see anyone come out. It took a few minutes to work out what happened. The bottom line is that now Joe had lost four hostages and a lot of time with nothing to show for his efforts.

Each released hostage was interviewed. They expressed sympathy for poor Joe and confirmed they had seen only one weapon. It was a pistol like the cowboys use. They were not sure of the caliber. A new plan was worked out that allowed someone to slide the patio door open and retrieve the package. As you might expect, Joe was upset because there was not enough money in the package. Dave told him the amount money was not important. What was important was the show of good faith by the police. Joe wanted money not expressions of good faith. He did not care if Dave was a Protestant or a Catholic, he wanted his money. Negotiations continued. It was becoming clear to Dave that Joe was not a rocket scientist.

I believe that by this time, it was learned that his car had been abandoned and since recovered by the police. This provided a positive identification of him from hostages C1–C4, who picked him out of a photo spread. He did not have a criminal history. However, from papers in his vehicle, previous employers were identified and interviewed. This provided excellent intelligence and gave Dave some insight into the type of person with whom he was dealing. In laymen's terms, it was decided that Joe should have an "L" for loser tattooed on his forehead.

During the course of the siege, one of the hostages, whose husband was the manager of a local hardware story, promised Joe a job. She felt very sorry for poor Joe, who was being used and abused by society. Finally, Joe announced he was going to fold his tent. Dave had been careful to avoid using terms suggesting defeat, like *surrender*. He suggested Joe "fold his tent" and exit the room. Joe agreed to fold his tent, but he wanted to do so within the room so his friends could watch and make sure the police did not hurt him. It took a few minutes for the tactical team to discuss and eventually approve this new plan. The plan involved Joe placing his pistol on a table, opening the drapes so police could see the weapon, and then move to the side of the room away from the pistol and his hostages. This plan was accomplished. The pistol was on one side near the hostages, and Joe was on the far side of the room.

The tactical team entered and began placing Joe under arrest. For reasons still not clear, they walked past the loaded pistol. During the arrest and pat down, the hostages yelled at the officers. They told them not to hurt Joe. Of course Joe was upset and gave the impression of being abused. It was then that one of them picked up the pistol and said something like, "Stop hurting him or I will start shooting you." This got their attention. For a moment that seemed like an eternity, there was a standoff. Then the hostage put down the weapon and began to cry. She later appeared with the police when they spoke to groups of potential hostages where she spoke of her trauma and reaction to the stress of captivity.

Joe was taken into custody, and Dave interviewed him. Dave wanted a statement, but Joe did not want to talk. The problem was that Joe did not have the courage to tell Dave he did not want to talk. So he remained passive and evasive and let Dave do all the work. So Dave, after the appropriate Miranda warning, said something like:

Dave: O.K. Joe, tell me in your own words what happened today.

Joe: (silence)

Dave: (Because his adrenalin level was still sky high, he decided to start the story in hopes that Joe would pick it up and continue.) "I understand you needed money for an operation on your son."

Joe: (Silence, then after a minute or two of silence that seemed like an eternity to Dave) Yep.

(Dave waited another eternity.) Joe said nothing.

Dave: You chose this hotel because you did some work there and knew they had a lot of cash on hand.

Joe: Yep.

I think you get the picture. We ended up with Detective Sergeant Dave Simpson confessing and periodically Joe saying yep. Joe was tried and convicted of attempted robbery. I do not know how much time he served.

Lessons Learned

1. Most psychologists call this passive aggressive behavior. It is common and normal in young children. In adults, it is abnormal. The person, patient, or prisoner gets his or her way by passively resisting attempts to push them in a direction he or she does not want to go and in so doing forces the other to do most of the work. Typically, he or she has been doing this for many years and becomes a proficient manipulator.
2. The tactical team learned to be more specific in assigning responsibilities for hostage control.

3. The negotiating team saw the effect and results of the Stockholm Syndrome as did the tactical officers.
4. The key was playing a waiting game to fatigue Joe. Although a rescue may have been possible, Joe was not threatening anyone and was slowly winding down.

Where Is Everybody?

There was an interesting case at the German consulate in an office building on Michigan Avenue in downtown Chicago that involved two Croatian subjects who, though politically motivated and considered terrorists, proved that one must not jump to the conclusion that terrorists are well organized, sophisticated, intelligent, or dedicated. The case began when a telephone call was received from the receptionist at the consulate who advised of the hostage taker's presence. A foreign consulate is, for lack of a better term, a business office for that nation in a foreign country. It helps tourists with visa applications and businesses that are engaged in various transactions with its government. A person who has the title of Consul General heads consulates. They have diplomatic status. Why these two knuckleheads chose the consulate in Chicago rather than the German embassy in Washington, D.C., is beyond me. Perhaps they lived closer to Chicago than to D.C.

Because of the involvement of German citizens, at least one of whom had diplomatic status, the FBI handled the case. The Chicago police helped evacuate and then secure the multistory office building. The subjects, who spoke English, were armed with revolvers and claimed to have a bomb. They waved the revolvers around, and the alleged bomb was in view on the floor near the hostages. Their only demand was that a fellow Croatian, who was in a German prison, be released and flown to Yugoslavia.

The negotiations process revealed that the terrorists were aware of the time difference among Chicago, Washington, D.C., and Bonn. However, they did not know in which German prison their friend was being held, and they were also unaware of German holidays. They came to the consulate the day before only to find it closed. The siege response from the Chicago Division of the FBI involved the positioning of a tactical team via a side door to the consulate office complex that led to a supply and storage area. However, the threat of a bomb was a factor for the tactical team to consider.

During the early stages of the siege, the subjects were identified, and appropriate search warrants were obtained for their homes and other locations to which they had access where bomb-making paraphernalia might be found. During the siege, the searches discovered no bomb-making paraphernalia. However, it is impossible to prove a negative, so we had to operate on the assumption that they might have explosives. It was learned that they had access to revolvers. They knew the name of their friend, but because they had no idea in which German prison he was incarcerated, time was needed, taken and gained as phone calls were made among Chicago, the Department of State (DoS) in Washington, D.C., the U.S. embassy in Bonn, and their calls to the appropriate German government offices involved. Further, they did not know the charges against him, his sentence, or how much longer he was to be incarcerated. As I recall, he was in prison because of a minor role he played in an unsuccessful Croatian attempt to shoot the Yugoslavian ambassador to Germany a few years before.

They knew his name, but its spelling was complex, unusual, and, I am sure, suffered some in the process of translation. Of course, that added to their unanticipated need for additional time. I am sure you are getting the message that "The devil is in the details." The resolution of these issues plus language differences and distances involved took time. Just getting started took so long that I was able to fly from Quantico to Chicago and drive to the consulate long before the negotiations process was in full swing. The not so good news is the Special Agent in Charge (SAC) in Chicago not only decided that he would negotiate, but he did so face to face with folks who claimed to have a bomb. In this process, he violated most of the FBI siege response rules. Try as we might, we could not dissuade him, and our calls to FBI headquarters for help went unheeded. We had a disaster in the making.

As this process dragged on into the night, the time difference between the cities became more of an issue. Yet somehow at some crazy early morning hour in Germany, their version of the Bureau of Prisons located the Croatian in question. He was advised of the situation in Chicago. He said he had no previous knowledge of their plan. In addition, he said he was sick and tired of crazy Croatian politics. He wanted to finish his sentence that was now down to about a year and wash his hands of all this Croatian craziness. It was his story, and we were stuck with it.

Frankly, if I were in a German prison, I too would wash my hands of foreign politics. As I recall, he had a German wife, and they had one child. This was good news for us. However, it took awhile to convince the two subjects of the facts. Finally, via a series of telephone connections, they were able to speak directly with their associate in Germany who told them in no uncertain terms to leave him alone. They surrendered. Their pistols were loaded. However, their bomb was a fake. They ended up in federal prison for several years, during which their friend was released from prison in Germany, found a job, and occupied himself with family matters not Croatian politics. I suspect his genuine cooperation in this case was a consideration in the timing of his early release.

Lessons Learned

1. We certainly learned not to make assumptions about the sophistication of those claiming to be terrorists.
2. It was gratifying to see firsthand just how much time can be involved in the most simple request response. We really did not have to stall for time. Their demands were such that a lot of time was required by our attempts to satisfy them.
3. I will give the SAC credit for his ability to convince these knuckleheads that we were doing the best we possibly could, but even doing our best was taking much longer than anyone anticipated.
4. The mistakes included the fact that as well as the SAC-handled negotiations, his job was the on-scene commander not a negotiator.
5. Time was used effectively to evaluate the demands and demeanor of the subjects.
6. Intelligence was gathered and used to frustrate and fatigue these two ill prepared subjects. As the negotiations process progressed, their lack of preparation became more and more evident.
7. Finally, the careful use of a TPI, their cousin in a German jail, convinced them to surrender. To the best of my knowledge, their jailed cousin was released a year or so after the siege and moved with his German wife back to what was Yugoslavia, where they lived happily ever after. Both subjects ended up in federal prison.

I Can See That

A few years ago, a 166-hour siege occurred in London from which we all learned some valuable lessons. As I recall, Scotland Yard referred to this case as "The Spaghetti House Siege." To clarify the time involved, there are 168 hours in a week. According to The Yard, the owners of several independent Italian restaurants in London decided to work together to increase their profits. One way to do this was to buy in bulk and then distribute the purchases themselves. An easy and enjoyable way to accomplish this was for the owners to meet about once a week at one of the restaurants, socialize, and eat dinner as they placed and paid for their orders. They ordered everything from tables to tomatoes to Tokay. Some local crooks learned of this through a family member who worked at one of the restaurants. During one of the meetings, the crooks broke in, took the owners hostage, and demanded their money. As I recall, this took place in the basement of the restaurant that had limited outside access. To set the stage: They were in a restaurant basement, with lots of food, and there were several crooks. All combined to add hours to the siege that lasted one week.

The owners, who were of Italian heritage, did not speak English very well. The Jamaican accents of the crooks made their proper English rather poor. Imagine the yelling and confusion of two groups speaking different versions of the same language. This noise, confusion, and delay in communication provided enough time for employees upstairs to contact the police, who quickly sealed off the basement, and the siege began.

Once trapped, the crooks decided they were not crooks but members of a Jamaican terrorist group known as The Black Liberation Army. Fortunately, the negotiators were well trained and knew of the New York incident at John and Al's Sporting Goods, where the crooks also decided they were more likely to be allowed to leave if the police believed they were terrorists. It did not work in New York or London. Frankly, I do not understand this thinking process. Of course, the problem may be these knuckleheads are incapable of thinking intelligently.

The negotiations were conducted via a telephone line. The line was controlled so the crooks could not make a call to anyone but the negotiator. As the crooks made demands for money and transportation, the negotiators listened and said they were doing all they could to comply. To allow themselves some freedom around the basement, the crooks tied the older owners to their chairs. During the siege, they told the negotiators they had tied up their hostages. The negotiators commented that the owners were really not a physical threat to them and that given their age and circulation problems, it might not be a good idea to leave them bound. This subject came up a few times during which the Yard's technical team was able to insert a visual probe through an air vent. The visual aid was available to command, tactical, intelligence, and, as it turned out, unfortunately to the negotiating element.

As negotiations progressed, the crooks said they would untie or at least loosen the ropes holding the older men to their chairs. The negotiators said that would be a good idea. Unfortunately, the negotiator was watching the subjects untie the owners as he was speaking with their spokesperson. This proved to be a bad idea. Later in negotiations, when they were discussing acts of good faith, the crooks said something like:

Crook: I told you we would loosen those ropes, and I am a man of my word. We untied them.

Negotiator: I can see that. (Not good. The crook immediately responded.)

Crook: You can see that?

Negotiator: What I meant was I believe what you said.

Crook: No you said you could see that. (In the search that followed, the crooks found the probe and engaged in a tug of war with a technician, the result of which deleted the visual aid and damaged the equipment.)

Eventually, the crooks surrendered and went off to "The Old Bailey."

Lessons Learned

1. Scotland Yard told the rest of us what happened. We all agreed that the negotiator does not really need direct access to intelligence probes. Each department came up with various ways of

handling such intelligence and how to filter it to the negotiating team.

Institutional Sieges

The majority of sieges that occur in prisons are the result of a foiled escape attempt or the need for better living conditions. While in graduate school, I did a two-semester, two-day-a-week internship as a parole agent with the California Department of Corrections (CDC). The CDC understood that the best ways to prevent riots and sieges were adequate food, decent clothing, and regular visiting privileges tied to the good behavior of the inmate.

My second year involved a full-time fall semester internship at the Atascadero State Hospital (ASH) for the Sexual Psychopath. At Atascadero, I learned that most behavior problems with patients began after a visit from a relative. Therefore, after visits, the patients were encouraged to meet with someone on the staff who would defuse their emotions and perhaps recommend a temporary change in medication. To the best of my knowledge, there has never been a siege at ASH or any other California state mental hospital.

The Long Lewis Lament

The state of Arizona has a seven-unit facility that houses 4,000 inmates in Buckeye, Arizona. It is located about fifty miles southwest of Phoenix south of I-10 on State Highway 85. One might say it is in the middle of nowhere. It was the site of the longest prison siege in U.S. history. It began with a foiled prison escape on Sunday, January 18, 2004, and ended some fifteen days later with the surrender of the two inmates on February 1 (Rapp & Davis, 2006).

You Can Kill Him Now

For a more detailed description of this siege from the perspective of a hostage, there is a book titled *Hostage: 15 Days in Hell.* It is the story of an employee hostage, Ms. Lois Fraley, and was published in California (Rapp & Davis, 2006).

Inmates have little to do, so they and their relatives spend an inordinate amount of time figuring out ways to get out of prison. In this case, the ill advised but eventually cooperative sister of one of the escapees ran a website for him proclaiming his innocence for dozens of charges to include those for which he was sentenced in Arizona. For those who want more information on this siege, the victim Lois Fraley is available to speak to groups and can be contacted via Google by typing Lois Fraley and then going to Lois Fraley hostage. That sequence will bring you to her website. I tried to no avail to bring up her website directly. She is running a nonprofit to help former hostages cope with the stress of their ordeal. I met and spoke with her at length in San Diego when she made a presentation to the California Association of Hostage Negotiators in May 2007. Much of the material presented here has been drawn from our conversations and her book.

The two subjects were cellmates serving long sentences for a series and variety of offenses. The leader was Ricky Wassenaar, who was a 40-year-old person with ASP. He was serving twenty-eight years for armed robbery and assault. In prison, he was known as "Rooster" who was a jailhouse bookie and lawyer.

His associate was Steven Michael Coy, also 40 and serving seven consecutive life sentences for crimes that included armed robbery and rape. His most recent offense involved his pregnant girlfriend who was waiting in the getaway car when the police arrived. He was delayed after the robbery because he decided to stick around and rape the owner's wife. Before he could get, out the police arrived and arrested him. Coy had roots in Maine. Wassenaar had roots in Michigan. His sister lived there and operated a website for him that proclaimed his innocence. The decision to assign them as cellmates turned out to be a bad idea.

They had been planning their escape for years. Their plan began on a Sunday morning when most of the experienced staff was off. During this critical incident, only one of the officers involved had more than sixteen months of experience in the unit. The subjects knew this and planned accordingly. As they anticipated, inexperienced staff did things they should not have, and the two escapees made it from the kitchen across the yard and into the Morey Tower where they held and abused hostages for two weeks. Wassenaar called it his tower and his fence. Typical of the ASP, he must be in charge (Dubina, 2012).

The secure tower had several shoulder weapons that included 1 AR 15, a Remington Shotgun and a 37 mm Gas gun (Dubina, 2012).

Negotiators and tactical units responded from across Arizona and, like the Hanaffi siege, many other states and levels of government. Their siege eventually cost the state of Arizona $3.6 million (Rapp & Davis, 2006).

Their initial demands included Wassenaar speaking to his sister, the governor and the media. He wanted an AM/FM radio, pizza and lasagna, an outside phone, and a helicopter.

Typical of the ASP, Ricky Wassenaar was out to get the best deal he could for himself. By day 13, the compact between Wassenaar and Coy appeared to be falling apart. Coy was willing to accept the deal and be transferred to Maine. Wassenaar was holding out for more. Therefore, to get more, Wassenaar tried to set up Coy for the kill. In his mind, this would make him look good to the authorities. Remember the motto for the ASP is "It's all about me." Wassenaar certainly lived up to that expression. His plan was for the authorities to kill Coy because, according to Wassennar, Coy would not accept the offer of an out-of-state transfer to a prison closer to Maine.

During what came to be called "The Whisper Negotiations," which are transcribed below, Wassenaar tried to get the authorities to kill Coy when he was on the Observation Deck. This area is also called the roof. Wassenaar finally convinced Coy to go out on the roof and take a look around. The negotiators then gave Wassenaar several options to surrender. They said things like "Close the hatch," "Walk out," and "Put both hands on the window" (Dubina, 2012). He would not. Because of tactical constraints, no shot was taken. The fear was that if Coy was shot, Wassenaar would kill the hostages inside with him.

Like many similar sieges, the inmates settled on day fifteen for what they had been offered on day four. Then Wassenaar changed his mind. Interestingly enough, when they did surrender, Coy pled guilty, took the out-of-state transfer, and is now serving seven life sentences in Maine. Wassenaar pled not guilty. Acting as his own attorney, he told the jury that it was not an attempted escape. It was his intent to demonstrate the inadequacies of the Lewis Prison. He wanted to help the state do a better job. The escape business was just a misunderstanding. In truth, Wassenaar was a dedicated public servant trying to do his civic duty. If you believe any of that, Jan Dubina has some ocean front property in south Phoenix for you at a great price (Dubina, 2012). In my experience, this is a common failing of ASPs. They are so convinced of their lies that they believe others will believe even the most ridiculous of stories.

Typical of an ASP, he pled not guilty and acted as his own attorney. Like most ASPs, he tried to paint the Arizona Department of Corrections as the culprit. That did not work. He was found guilty on nineteen of the twenty counts against him. He is now serving more than 400 years in an Ohio prison. Sixteen of his nineteen convictions carry life sentences. He will serve them consecutively after finishing his current sentence of twenty-eight years for the Tucson robbery.

Of the two weeks of negotiations, the following material is typical of ASPs and their "It's all about me" attitude (Roland, 2003). They will sell anyone else down the river if it is to their immediate and personal advantage. The conversation that reflects the ASP of Wassenaar (W) best is the one where he tried to convince the authorities to kill his partner Coy. It was on day 13. The negotiators (N) called this the whispered negotiations. He tried to convince the authorities to kill Coy because Coy wanted to kill Lois.

W: Hello. Bob?

N: uhm . . . this is Dan. I talked to you a couple of days ago. Uhm, when Bob, when Chuck wasn't here. But Bob's not in yet.

W: All right.

N: Did you just want to talk to Bob?

W: Tell everyone who calls to speak very softly.

N: Speak softly?

W: Yes, very softly.

N: O.K.

W: At, at a whisper.

N: At a whisper?

W: Yes.

N: O.K. How come?

W: Because I can hear you very clearly, we may have a problem here.

N: They have a problem?

N: Inter . . .

N: Inter problem?

W: Yes.

N: What do you mean by that?

W: A problem within the tower.

N: O.K.

W: Between the two captives . . . between the two captives . . . between the two captor.

N: O.K. is there anything I can help you with?

W: I'll speak with ah . . . him I guess.

N: With Bob?

W: Yes

N: O. K.

W: But, ah, tell him to speak very, very softly. Can you hear me?

N: I hear you.

W: All right.

N: I hear you . . . it will not be too long . . . ah, umm . . . how . . . does she need, you know, ah . . . does she have enough to drink and everything?

W: She's fine.

N: O.K. Ah, who is this? Is this Rick?

W: Yes.

N: O.K. all right. Is there anything else, ah, you want me to pass on to Bob?

W: I wanna make the deal. But . . . boy doesn't and ah . . . were gonna have a (inaudible) dead on you. He's determine to die in here.

N: O.K. (The reason for this reply was the negotiating team knew that Coy was ready to surrender and take the offer to be moved to a prison in Maine. It was obvious to all that Wassenaar was up to something.)

W: And he doesn't want to make any deal and ah . . . we have a pact together that ah . . . .he wasn't going to give up from the beginning before any of this started and if I break the pack it's gonna come to a gun battle between him and me.

N: O.K. How, how can we get you out?

W: We can't.

N: O.K. How can we do it?

W: We can't 'cause if we get me out, the female is dead. He's going to kill the female.

N: O.K.

W: So pass that along. Be sure to pass that along to Bob. I want to come out, but I can't do it because he's going to kill the female. He is not going to come out of here alive. And if he does, it's gonna be with the death penalty because he is going to kill the female.

N: O. K. Understand. We need you to think . . . O.K.? We need you to talk to him about how . . . we can help you come out.

W: The only way you can get me outta here and get her outta here alive is to kill him. That's the only way.

N: O.K.

W: The only way to get us out is to kill him.

N: O.K. I understand what you're saying.

W: Otherwise we're all gonna die in here.

N: We definitely don't want that. We want to help you.

W. Well, that's the situation. He is not going to take the deal. He is going to kill the female. And it's going to happen . . . pretty fucking soon.

N: O.K.

W: Maybe not today . . . maybe not. I don't know. Maybe today. Maybe tomorrow. I don't know.

N: O.K. But, but you don't want that.

W: I cannot talk him out. I cannot talk him out of anything.

N: O.K. But you want to come out.

W: Yeah.

N: O.K. We, we can work this out.

W: Coy does not. I cannot leave here. He will kill the female.

N: O.K.

W: If I leave the female dies immediately.

N: O.K. Then you need to be with Lois for the time being. We're gonna try. We're gonna try to help you. Do you have any ideas?

W: I'm thinking (inaudible) because he doesn't go up on the roof. He doesn't go up on the tower. I'm gonna try and get him up on the tower, and you guys are gonna kill him.

N: O.K. But if he won't go up there, what can we do?

W: If he don't go up there, he's gonna kill her. Probably me as well. He's gonna kill everybody.

N: You're going to release her?

W: No . . . he is gonna kill. There is no way that she can be released with him alive. Period.

The negotiators knew Wassenaar was the leader and Coy was the follower. So they played along with this story to see where it would end. Shortly after this exchange, for the first time Coy went out onto the tower roof. He briefly raised his arms and hands in a surrendering motion. He looked around and then went back in. While Coy was on the roof, the negotiator gave Wassenaar the options of closing and locking the hatch or running out the bottom door with Lois. He did not accept them. He wanted Coy shot so he could emerge as the hero who saved the female. Note that throughout the negotiations, Wassenaar referred to Lois as the female. He did his best to depersonalize her. For the ASP, people are to be used and abused by them for their purposes. In fact, they are the predators on the people we have sworn to protect and serve.

Lessons Learned

1. The Arizona Department of Corrections learned that the improper staffing of a prison with a disproportionate number of inexperienced staff on that Sunday morning. As Christians we appreciate and celebrate Sunday. Felons do not. The inmates knew this and took advantage of this experience weakness.
2. Inmates think about and plan their escape 24/7, while staff think about it 8/5. In addition, prisons are designed to keep people in, and the tower is designed to keep people out. They also serve to keep staff out of secure areas. That was the case in Arizona and every prison siege I have studied. History suggests that all too often these sieges must run their course.
3. Typically running their course includes the abuse of their hostages. During the February 2–3, 1980, New Mexico siege, prisoners killed thirty-three of their peers. Of the twelve staff taken hostage, some were abused and none was killed. The inmates wanted to tell the world they are the real victims of an unfair system. That was the case in New Mexico and twenty-four years later in Arizona.

There is a good book on the New Mexico siege titled *Descent into Madness: An Inmate's Experience of the New Mexico State Prison Riot.* It has an excellent introduction written by Mark Colvin, professor of sociology at George Mason University (Rolland, 1997).

Deadly Combination

No one is perfect. Just as physically one can have a broken arm and a tooth ache, so it is with mental maladies. Mental health professionals, many of whom are members of the American Psychological Association (APA), have long understood that some people have more than one malady.

Such was the case with the person discussed here who was previously imprisoned and labeled by prison psychologists, who tested and observed him over several years, as an ASP who was also bipolar. One is a personality disorder like the obsessive compulsive or narcissistic person. They are not crazy. They drive other people crazy with their obsession with order or self-centered lifestyle. Legally, they are held responsible for their actions. They are not out of touch with reality. The other, bipolar, is on the APA list of psychotic conditions. Legally speaking, psychotic people are insane. A major problem faced when dealing with people who are psychotic (AKA) is that some have bouts of sanity. In other words, many are not out of touch with reality or insane 24/7.

To help clarify psychological terms, the person who is now labeled bipolar was once called manic depressive. I prefer the manic depressive name because to me it is more descriptive. Their symptoms range from deep depression to hyper and prolonged physical activity. Further, and like physical ailments, there are degrees of mental illness. Just as one can have a slight cold or pneumonia, a person with a mental illness can be slightly or seriously psychotic. In addition, we all have mood swings. There are two fundamental differences between our mood swings and those of the bipolar. The primary difference is ours are based on reality, not chemically driven. In other words, normal people are depressed or elated because of recent events. The person with a bipolar is depressed or elated because of an internal chemical imbalance or fluctuation. The other difference is the extreme degree of their mood swings. On a scale of 1–10, a normal is 5. Our swings may go as low as three or as high as seven. Their swings can range from 1 to 10 and very often go off the scale at both ends.

In my judgment, this is the worst combination of mental maladies that a crisis response team can face. I say that because this person is an ASP, therefore he or she has no conscience, and typically the bipolar aspect of their illness provides them with a lot of energy. By that I mean they can stay awake for days. The siege discussed below lasted 96 hours. That was four days of negotiations. We do not know how long he was awake before the siege began. We suspect that was at least two days.

A hostage siege that featured a person who was a bipolar ASP was an exhausting experience for all involved. As I discussed at the beginning of Chapter 2, the ASP considers people as property. When one is involved with an ASP, you, in his or her mind, become property. This is an important concept and mind-set to remember. It is probably the root cause for the four-day siege that occurred in a suburb of Baltimore a few years ago.

You Belong to Me

Late one afternoon, a man I will call Moe located his girlfriend Stacey, who had recently terminated their relationship. She dared to leave him and was living with friends. He figured out where she was and broke into their apartment. He shot and killed her unarmed elderly friends as they were talking with Stacey in their living room. He dragged her out the door. A neighbor in the apartment complex heard her screams and stepped into the hall to investigate. Moe shot and killed him. Moe threw Stacey into his car and drove off. Neighbors who heard the shots and screaming called the police. They knew the story about Moe and told the police he was probably the person who did the shooting. The DMV provided a photo and vehicle description. So the search began.

He soon abandoned the car and attempted to steal a vehicle by shooting and killing the driver. He eventually stole a car from a little old lady. During all this, he dragged Stacey along with him . . . after all she was his property. That night he checked them into a local motel. In the process of checking in, Stacey spotted two uniformed officers and ran to them screaming for help. They protected her. Moe ran away. It was later learned that he made his way south into Stafford County, Virginia. That is the site of the FBI Academy, about fifty miles south of Washington, D.C., which is about fifty miles south of Baltimore. So he was about one hundred miles south of the crime scene.

Stacey was provided with police protection. She stayed at their department and lived in a holding cell for almost a week. They left her door unlocked, but in anticipation of his return to pick up his proper-

ty, her movement was restricted, and extra officers with shoulder weapons were positioned in and around the police station. By this time,
the police and FBI had completed some background checks on Moe
and learned he had previously held hostages in Montana. During that
siege, he made many promises that he did not keep. The Montana tactical team was able to make an entry and arrested Moe. He spent a few
years in their state prison. Yet he, like most ASPs, was a very likeable
and gregarious person who charmed his way out of prison and later
out of more and more trouble.

To no avail, the police continued their search of southern Maryland and offered to protect Stacey's family. They declined the offer. As
expected, Moe decided to return from Virginia to Maryland to claim
his property. He took her parents and younger brother hostage in their
two-story row house. So the siege began. He took them hostage and
called the police to announce his presence, the identity of his hostages,
and his demand that Stacey be brought to him. During negotiations,
Moe frequently fired at the police and FBI. Many of the neighbors
were evacuated to a local school. Police and FBI negotiators, tactical,
intelligence, and command elements worked around the clock day
after day for almost a week.

Unfortunately, before all of their land and cellular lines were captured, Moe contacted a local TV station. He told them he just wanted
to go on the air and speak with Stacey. He said he did not mean to kill
those four people. I guess in his mind this meant he was not really
guilty of multiple homicides. The newsperson with whom he was
speaking told him the station did not have the capability of patching
through the phone line to the studio for a live discussion. During that
conversation, the FBI intercepted and controlled the telephone lines
from the house. Now Moe could only talk with the authorities.

A little later, Moe told the negotiators he would kill Stacey's young
brother if Stacey was not put on the phone. The negotiators tried to
convince him that they did not know where she was. They told him
she ran away from the police who had given him chase at the motel.
Moe did not believe them and began a countdown, saying when he
reached zero he would kill her brother. Negotiators pleaded with him
to wait. He kept counting. Negotiators were told that the tactical team
did not at that time have an entry plan with which they were comfortable. He kept counting. The negotiators had been told that Moe real-

ly liked her younger brother, yet he kept counting. The negotiations process went something like:

Moe: I want you to bring Stacey to the phone or I am going to kill her brother.

PD: I will see what I can do to locate her.

Moe: I guess you did not hear me. If she is not brought to the phone, I am going to shoot him.

PD: I heard you, and I have placed a call to command to find her.

Moe: You are lying to me. Ten. When I get to one I will shoot him.

PD: Even if I knew where she was, it would take time to get her here.

Moe: Nine.

PD: Moe, this hard-line approach will not accomplish anything.

Moe: Eight.

PD: You have got to understand this is a major operation. Even if she were here, getting her to this phone would take time.

Moe: Seven.

PD: We have been talking for several hours, and I know you are smart enough to understand that shooting John will not accomplish anything positive.

Moe: Six.

And so it went until Moe got to one. Then he fired a shot. Moments that seemed like an eternity passed before a "stand-off" listening device picked up the voice of her young brother saying he should have covered his ears better. Everyone on site breathed a sigh of relief.

Negotiations, or more accurately his ranting, continued day after day. Finally, Moe fell asleep. Stacey's parents escaped out the back door. Seeing this, the tactical team made an emergency entry. They swarmed through the row house and found Moe upstairs. They shot and killed him as he reached for one of his weapons.

Lessons Learned

1. The practice of working in shifts over the four days was perfected.
2. Good intelligence flow between the shifts and teams was achieved.
3. Time allowed for intelligence on Moe to be gathered and analyzed. This intelligence came from people and authorities in Idaho and Montana with whom Moe had previously negotiated, his former girlfriend, and other associates. It was feared that if Stacey was put on the phone with Moe, he would say something like "See what you have made me do." And then shoot her parents.
4. It was the escape of two of the three hostages that forced the hand of the police. Fortunately, and because they had used time so well, an emergency assault/rescue plan had been practiced to perfection on a similarly configured home. John was rescued.
5. The negotiations process bought time for intelligence to be gathered so the on-scene commander could make the right decision. It was the "gut feeling" of many officers and agents on scene that Moe would not surrender. It turns out they were right. However, the on-scene commander should not make life-and-death decisions based on "gut feelings."

In Summary

The intent of this chapter was to identify and discuss a variety of sieges from which many lessons were learned that could be generalized to a variety of settings. The person I labeled as Bad is typically a criminal with a history of offenses who most frequently has an ASP. They are not crazy. They just don't care about anyone but themselves. Their life motto is "It's all about me." The examples discussed showed that this personality disorder may be seen in preteen years through adulthood. To effectively deal with the ASP, the negotiator must understand their two common defense mechanisms of projection ("It ain't my fault") and rationalization ("Everyone does it"). In addition, people with this disorder who are intelligent can put a crisis response team through a stressful few hours or days. Because many people so labeled are soothing their hostages tend to side with them. This can create problems for the response team. I included one example that could be labeled a terrorist incident. In the United States we have avoided the label of terrorist and have instead focused on the criminal act they are committing. We negotiate with them as criminals, not social, political, or religious reformers.

I discussed only one institution siege. That is because published examples about such sieges are generally and necessarily vague. Inmates tend to have access to such write-ups and can make an institutional siege more difficult than it need be. Most correctional institutions and jails learn the details of sieges from those who participated or were victimized when they make presentations to selected audiences. Finally, and by way of introduction to the next chapter, a hostage taker who had an ASP and was also bipolar, a psychotic condition, was discussed.

References

Babiak, P., & Hare, R. D. PhD. (2006). *Snakes in suits.* New York: Harper Collins.

City of Winterhaven v. Allen. (1989). 5412 So 2nd 128 (Fla. App.).

Downs v. United States. (1983). 382. F. Supp. 752.

Dubina, J. (2012). Personal interview at the Negotiator Competition, Southwest Texas State University, San Marcos, Texas, January 11.

Goergen, M. (2010). *Crisis negotiators field guide.* Eagle Training, Minneapolis, MN.

Hare, R. D. (1993). *Without conscience.* New York: Guilford Press.

Harris, T. A. (1967). *I'm OK–You're OK.* New York: Avon Books, New York

Machiavelli, N. (1948). *The prince.* New York: Appleton-Greenwood Press.

Moon v. W. (1974). 388 F. Supp31, (N.D. Ill.)

Noesner, G. (2010). *Stalling for time.* New York: Random House.

Rapp, K., & Davis, R. (2006). *Hostage: 15 Days in Hell: An account of the longest prison hostage siege in United States history.* Garden Grove, CA: Printmediabooks.

Roland, J. (2003, May 28). *Assessing the Hostage Taker from a Mental Health Professionals Perspective.* Presentation to the California Association of Hostage Negotiators, Annual Training Conference, Long Beach, CA.

Rolland, M. (1997). *Descent into madness: An inmate's experience of the New Mexico state prison riot.* Cincinnati, OH: Anderson Publishing.

Strentz, T. (2012). *Psychological aspects of crisis negotiations* (2nd ed.). Boca Raton, FL: CRC Press.

Chapter 3

THE MAD

The siege subjects I find easy to deal with are those who are legally insane, psychologically psychotic, and generically mad who are usually suffering from paranoid schizophrenia. Perhaps this is because my earliest experience with severely disordered minds was with psychotic patients at ASH. I learned the importance of listening. Perhaps that is because we did not know how to cure them, so my first job was to monitor their mien so we could prescribe the least amount of medication possible to help them manage their behavior.

For the purposes of this chapter and generally speaking, these three words, *insane, psychotic,* and *mad,* are synonyms.

I will never forget one patient at Atascadero who sang his version of a then popular Perry Como song, "Wake the Town and Tell the People." This patient sang his version called "Wake the Town and Kill the People." He had a wonderful baritone voice; the terracotta tile corridors of the hospital resonated his musical efforts like a large shower stall. Were it not for his insane choice of lyrics, I think he could have sold many records. I never met him, I knew him only by his voice.

I had my own groups of psychotic patients, all of whom were paranoid schizophrenic sex offenders, none of whom could sing very well. I learned early in my internship that the best way to deal with these patients was to let them tell their story and in that process listen for clues to possible cures and control. **Control** because one of the treatment goals was limiting the amount of prescribed medication. Most psychotropic drugs have side effects that range from discomfort to death. One way to limit the complications of such side effects is to keep the dosage at the lowest level possible. Dr. Anderson told me during our first meeting that we could not cure psychotic patients of their mental malady because we did not know the cause. He said our treatment options were then, and unfortunately remain today, treating the symptoms. Medically speaking, that is like a doctor treating a patient suffering from Tuberculosis (TB) by prescribing a cough suppressant. They stop coughing, but the TB continues unabated. As it was in 1965 it remains today—we treat the symptoms of delusions and hallucinations but not their cause. Further, the debate over nature or nurture, heredity versus environment continues.

The lone exception is with manic-depressive/bipolar patients. With them there is excellent evidence suggesting heredity. Typically a Lithium derivative is prescribed with good results. The major problem with Lithium is just a little too much is fatal. The problem encountered when negotiating with a person who has a bipolar disorder is that the negotiator, at one extreme, is trying to waltz with a whirling dervish and, at the other extreme, trying to dance with the dead. What works best is just letting them talk until they are worn out. This can take days. The other tactic is getting them back on their meds. However, even that takes time. Their medication does not usually take immediate effect. So again we face the edict of Gary Noesner of avoiding the action imperative and stalling for time (Noesner, 2010).

Symptoms

Simply stated, psychotic people typically have two primary symptoms: **delusions** and **hallucinations**. A **delusion** is a false belief. Typically, there are two types of delusions—delusions of grandeur and delusions of persecution. Some argue that all are delusions of grandeur because only important people are persecuted. Therefore, both are basically delusions of grandeur. Be that as it may, a delusion is a false belief that is held in spite of good evidence to the contrary.

A **hallucination** is a misperception of reality. We have five senses. The term *hallucination* has five syllables. A hallucination is a "miss reading" of one or more of the senses. The most common is the report of hearing voices. The least common is seeing things. Between these two are reports of feeling, smelling, and tasting things that are not reality. When I write *feeling* I do not mean an emotional response. I mean touch or tactile like "feeling" your skin is crawling.

Listen and Learn

Because of Dr. Anderson's words, I listened to my patients and provided reality checks for them and, in the process, monitored the effectiveness of their medication. Again, maintaining the proper prescription level of anti-psychotic medication is important because most of them have unpleasant side effects. One way to ameliorate these side effects is to keep the level of the drug as low as possible. The movie "A Beautiful Mind" depicted one side—impotence. Another motive for the treatment was to gauge the reality level of the patient to determine whether he, like Dr. John Nash as portrayed by Russell Crowe in "A Beautiful Mind," was marginally insane and able to respond to logic. In that movie, his roommate and the little girl were very real to him as they were to the audience until the very end, when it was clear both people were fictitious. That is to say, they were hallucinations. However, just as we in the audience believed they were real, so too does the psychotic person believe in their reality. What this all means for the process of crisis negotiations is a good negotiating tactic is to just listen. That is what the FBI, the Prince George's and Phoenix Police Departments and others did effectively in the cases discussed below.

Benny, the All American Boy

There is a large mall in Prince George's County, Maryland, that is northeast of Washington, D.C. It was at this mall that the Prince George's County Police Department responded to and effectively negotiated with a mentally ill man who had a bomb and several hostages. Maryland, unlike California and most states, has county police departments. They are the primary law enforcement department in the county. The Sheriff's Department provides courtroom security and serves warrants and other civil papers like eviction notices.

This crisis response began when the receptionist in the Maryland Department of Employment called 911 at around 2:00 p.m. in early February to report a man with a bomb was seated at her desk in their foyer. This office is located in a large mall. There is only one way in or out, and it had thick inoperable windows. The receptionist did an excellent job of keeping him in the foyer while about a dozen employees and visitors were trapped in the offices behind her.

Her first clue that something was wrong came when Benny, who was carrying a briefcase with a protruding switch, asked her whether she spoke English. She said she did and asked him how she could help. He said he was glad that an Iranian spoke such good English, and he told her he had several demands. The first responding officers found a list of his demands in a briefcase. Benny left that briefcase in the elevator. His list of demands included that a local radio station play every David Bowie song except "Blue, Blue, Electric Blue." In addition, he wanted a quart of ice tea (Maryland in February is characterized by damp cold air and not a time when people consume a lot of ice tea), immunity from prosecution, enforcement of his civil rights, deportation to any country that would accept him, and all signings of documents granting these demands to be witnessed and aired by a local radio station. This is certainly a mixed bag of demands.

During his initial discussion, it became clear that he thought he was in the Iranian embassy. At that time, there was no Iranian embassy in Washington, D.C. That was another clue. He told her he had bombs in the briefcase he was holding and wanted to change things quickly. The police response was immediate because of the prompt reaction of mall security officers who called the police. The first responding patrol officer engaged Benny in a voice-to-voice conversation from just outside the foyer door. This distraction allowed the receptionist an opportunity to move back into the office and join the others. Soon the siege response team arrived and negotiations began.

The negotiations continued down the track initiated by the first responder, who introduced the negotiator and then went to the command post to be debriefed. Benny told the trained negotiator, Corporal Bill Hogewood, he had a bomb. He said he knew it worked because he had practiced. Bill played dumb about bombs to draw Benny out. He used open-ended questions and other active listening skills as Bill kept Benny talking about his bomb. Like most "bombers," Benny was proud of what he built. Benny said he learned how to make a bomb in a Texas mental hospital by a bomber who had set off many bombs in and around Austin, Texas. Because Benny said he had practiced, this intelligence was passed on, and additional information was gathered about Benny.

Back at the police station, a review of recent complaints revealed several reports of explosions. The EOD (Explosive Ordance Disposal) team that investigated the calls determined the size and type of explosive used. Once again, the neighborhood around the vacant lots where most of the explosions had occurred was covered and people were questioned. A woman reported that she had seen Benny leave his home that morning with a briefcase. When she asked him where he was going, he told her he was going to the Iranian embassy. She knew Benny was a troubled young man whose parents were responsible middle-class federal employees. They were contacted at work and said that each night they secured their bedroom door to protect themselves from Benny. A few years ago, they had finally succeeded in having him institutionalized. He ended up in a Texas mental hospital. But against their wishes, he was released. They authorized a search of his room. Bomb-making paraphernalia was found, as was residue from the type of bombs that had exploded around the neighborhood over the past few months. It certainly appeared that Benny had a bomb. Given this intelligence and the fact that he thought he was at the Iranian embassy strongly suggested that he was at best disoriented and possibly insane. So, the police were facing a crazy person in a large shopping mall who had a workable bomb. Isn't that a delightful combination?

It was decided to distract Benny so contact could be made with the people in the offices behind him. He was told to ignore the ringing telephone because those calls had nothing to do with him. He complied. Fortunately, the employees hiding in the back offices answered their phone, and contact was made and maintained with them. That line remained open. All the others were cut. Of course, that created problems for the media that had descended on the mall like bees around honey. This kept the Public Information Officer very busy.

The negotiator, then Cpl. Bill Hogewood, did an outstanding job engaging Benny in long conversations about communists, Iranians, the Viet Cong, and whatever Benny wanted to discuss. Notice the discussions paraphrased below slip back and forth between rational conversations and discussions of his delusions. In reality, they were delusions. To Benny (B), they were reality, his reality with and about which Bill (BH) had to converse and cope.

BH: Benny?

B: Go ahead.

BH: Just checking out the equipment to make sure it is working.

B: O.K.

BH: Don't worry about those other phones. Listen, I want you to promise me something.

B: O.K.

BH: I want you to sit right there in that chair. O.K.?

B: Uh-Huh. Why is it loaded?

BH: No it's not loaded.

B: O.K.

BH: Are you having trouble hearing me?

B: Turn up the amplifier.

BH: Maybe you know how to operate this equipment.

B: You mean this isn't the Iranian embassy?

BH: You know where you're at don't you?

B: I think those people back there are Viet Cong sympathizers.

BH: What do you think about letting those people go now?

B: They're Viet Cong sympathizers.

BH: Benny, we discussed that already.

B: Are you going to let those Russians and communist Chinese take over this country?

BH: Nobody is going to bother you.

B: I'm running for public office.

BH: Public office.

B: Yea. I am running for Imperial King.

BH: Imperial King?

B: Ah, yeah of the world. World domination.

BH: World domination sounds impressive.

B: Yeah, I will collect taxes from everyone.

BH: What would you do with the taxes?

B: Ah, let me see. I'd find something to do with them. (crying)

BH: What's the matter?

B: Bill, will you give me immunity from prosecution?

This was the first indication that at some level he was thinking about surrender. He called the negotiator by his first name, and the his tone of voice changed. Notice how his thought process swings from logical to illogical. The good news during seven hours of negotiations is that Benny never made any direct threats to kill.

While Benny was talking with Bill, the tactical team was consulting with the folks who manage the mall to figure out a way to rescue the hostages hiding in the back of the office. There were external windows, but they were sealed and made of thick glass. Plus, opening or breaching those windows in February would immediately alert Benny of their actions and could result in him "pulling the pin." The front door was not an option because Benny was sitting there speaking with Bill. They considered cutting a hole into the space of the employment office from an adjoining business. Tests were conducted on similar walls to determine how quietly the cut could be made. The results were positive but discouraging. It was eventually determined that the only way to cut without Benny hearing the noise was for him to be sitting closer to the door and therefore closer to Bill who was engaging him in conversation.

Obviously going face to face with a psychotic person armed with a functioning bomb is not as safe as talking to him on the phone from across the parking lot. Further, the use of ballistic clothing would not provide much protection at such close range. This was "pucker time." Bill agreed that it was the only logical way to distract Benny and rescue the dozen hostages. Like friends of mine who won the Medal of Honor, Bill now refers to his decision and action as evidence of temporary insanity. Bill called Benny to ask him whether he would be comfortable with a face-to-face talk. Unfortunately for Bill, Benny said yes. It took a few minutes to work out the details, but Bill had won the confidence of a person suffering from paranoid schizophrenia. That is no simple task and remains a credit to his ability to communicate his sincere desire to help Benny. Like Dr. Anderson at Atascadero, Bill has winning ways about him that were easily communicated to troubled minds.

So they met in the mall just outside the office that Benny had occupied. They talked about whatever Benny wanted to discuss. While engaged in a time-consuming diversionary conversation, Bill also used the opportunity to try to convince Benny to "throw in the towel."

Even after Bill knew the hostages had been evacuated, he continued to talk with Benny who had his briefcase bomb in his lap. Benny kept his finger on the trigger that EOD had determined was a "dead man's switch." He and Bill kept talking about whatever Benny wanted to discuss. Bill eventually convinced him to come out. He did and was taken into custody. It turned out the bomb was real. It was exploded in an on-scene bomb detonation trailer.

In a post-incident interview with Bill, Benny told him that he had rigged his brother's electric razor to explode when he turned it on to shave. The brother was immediately notified, and an EOD team went to his residence and defused the bomb that, in their judgment, would have exploded and probably blown off his brothers head as Benny had planned.

Bill believes that Benny wanted to die that day at the mall. This conclusion is based on his use of an explosive device with an additional triggering mechanism tied to his neck. Plus, Benny told Bill his plan was to blow his own head off.

Lessons Learned

1. It is important for the negotiator to communicate sincere interest in the subject and his story. Bill accomplished this goal by agreeing with Benny at every logical opportunity. The key phrase is "logical opportunity." When mentally ill people talk about their hallucinations and ask you, as Benny did, if Bill saw the watermelons on the wall, the answer is not yes. A good answer is, "No, but I understand that you do. Tell me about them." I learned at Atascadero during my meetings with psychotic

patients who from time to time tested me to see if I was sincere. As mentioned above and evidenced by the conversation with Benny, some psychotic people slip in and out of a psychotic state. Some understand that what they see, hear, feel, taste, or smell is not real. However, at some level, it is real to them.

2. Do not confuse mental illness with intelligence. They are as different from each other as acne is from athlete's foot.

3. Bill evidenced concern for Benny. This concern allowed him to trust Bill with his life and eventually defuse his bomb and come out.

4. Certainly, the intelligence gathered by others on the department and other law enforcement agencies was crucial, as was the contact with the subject's parents and search of the house. I do not believe one can ever have enough intelligence on a subject. It is important to differentiate between what we know versus what we think we know.

5. The first responder remained with the negotiations think tank. As the negotiations progressed, he remembered more and more about his contact with Benny.

Islamic-Insane-Evil?

This siege occurred more than thirty-nine hours during March 9–11, 1977. It remains the longest, largest, and potentially the most dangerous and deadly hostage siege ever initiated on American soil. In quick summary, it involved three sites, 149 hostages, and twelve subjects, and it effectively paralyzed our nation's capital during the visit of then-Prime Minister Yitzhak Rabin from Israel.

This complex story involves a mad man who effectively led his youthful followers to avenge the deaths of six family members and a friend four years before. The siege began at about 1000 on March 9 when several men armed with swords ran from a Hertz rental truck they parked in front of B'nai B'rith, the eight-story international headquarters of a Jewish Social Service Organization near Du Pont Circle at 1640 Rhode Island Avenue N.W. in Washington, D.C. They carried supplies into the building and severely wounded several employees who were in the lobby. Most of them managed to escape.

The Washington, D.C., Metropolitan Police Department (MPD) was immediately called. It dispatched a unit that was two blocks away assisting the Secret Service detail providing security for the Prime Minister of Israel.

The unit arrived in minutes and observed the empty Hertz rental truck and people fleeing the building. Some of them were bleeding profusely. These facts were reported, and several other units were dispatched. The fact that the building under siege was a Jewish social service site and their prime minister was in town seemed like an ominous coincidence. To complicate matters, some of the people running from the building were employed in their sheltered workshop and had mental problems. When officers who did not know their mental health history interviewed some of them, they told bizarre stories of rape, murder, and mutilation. More reliable witnesses reported hearing the Negro male attackers yelling "Jihad, Jihad" as they forced people into elevators. It appeared to them that the elevators were going to the eighth floor, which is the top floor of the building. Gradually, all of the attacking Negro males left the lobby, and some employees who had been hiding exited the building. They provided additional intelligence on the number of subjects and the leadership role of the older male. One of them reported that immediately after the Hertz rental truck stopped, a Yellow Cab dropped off an older Negro male who took charge of the younger males.

To complicate matters, a little later at 1230, the police received a call from the Islamic Center on Massachusetts Avenue N.W. about six miles from Du Pont Circle. The caller said that two armed men had taken several people hostage in this facility that served the Washington, D.C., Moslem devout as a Mosque and museum. Units were immediately dispatched and verified that a siege was in progress at that location. The number and identity of the hostages, if any, were not immediately known.

At 1354, a call was received from a pay phone in the District Building, the Washington, D.C., equivalent of City Hall that is about a block from the White House. The caller said armed men had invaded the building, and shots had been fired. It was not immediately known how many men were involved or who, if anyone, had been hit, where they went, or who they were. At 1401, a second call from the District Building was received. The caller said he was helping prepare for the weekly city council meeting on the sixth floor. His office was near the elevators. He heard some shots. He saw two armed men running from the elevator. He reported that one city council member had been wounded, and a young man, who was bleeding profusely, was lying on the floor near the elevators. This caller said he was currently hiding under his desk.

MPD units were dispatched and observed many people running from the one block square and multistory District Building. Officers entered the building and, though under fire, evacuated those who had been shot. They knew the layout of the building and reported the shots came from the office of a city council member up the hall from the elevators at the opposite end of the floor from the large city council meeting room. Other officers were immediately dispatched and via some back stairs were able to secure the meeting room. The two shooters were isolated at the far end of the corridor now controlled by them. The only exit for them was toward the meeting room, and the police positioned to prevent such a move. It was not immediately known whether the gunmen had any hostages. The city council member in whose office they had taken refuge was with his staff in the council chamber. It appeared that the gunmen, if it was their intent to take the City Council hostage, had taken a wrong turn when exiting the elevator. The MPD first responders had secured the scene and were soon replaced by a tactical element with heavier weapons.

We had a city, our nation's Capital, under siege. Congress adjourned, some ceremonies at the White House were cancelled, and many federal employees were sent home as law enforcement tried to "get a handle" on these events. Drawing on Memos of Understand and Mutual Aid agreements, many officers responded from surrounding jurisdictions to guard potential targets and relieve MPD officers after their long shifts. By early afternoon, we had a city, our nation's capitol that was then playing host to the prime minister of Israel at the White House, involved in three siege sites. We were under siege as we reacted and prepared for the next target to go down. Fortunately, they stopped at three. At one the hostages were predominantly Jewish, at the second the hostages were predominantly Moslem, and at the third the hostages were predominantly Christian. Some early speculation concluded the three sites were under the control of a Satanic Cult. We were half right—it was a cult.

The MPD was on the case and provided the early and most accurate intelligence on this crisis. Hertz and the Yellow Cab companies were quickly contacted. The cab company reported the fare dropped at B'nai B'rith had been picked up at 7700 16th Street N.W., Washington, D.C. The credit card used to rent the truck was listed to Hamaas Abdul Khaalis at the same address. This was the foundation for the three day intelligence gathering mission for the Washington, D.C., crisis response team that soon involved every law enforcement agency in the metropolitan area, the military, federal agencies, bureaus, and departments that included human and intelligence resources from the federal government. I was there and know it was a "full court press."

The records of the MPD revealed the residence at 7700 16th Street N.W. was the subject of many calls for service. It was owned by Mr. Khaalis and served as the headquarters for his Islamic sect known as the Hanafi Moslems. In fact, Hanafi Moslems are part of the Sunni Sect and are no more involved in or at this address than is any local Lutheran Church. For reasons that remain unclear, Mr. Khaalis chose this name to identify his group and in so doing separate himself and his followers from the "Black Moslems" with whom he had been involved.

A review of MPD calls revealed that Mr. Khaalis had made many threats against several Jewish leaders in the Washington, D.C., metropolitan area whom he said were involved in a conspiracy with Malcolm X, the leader of "The Black Moslems," headquartered in Chicago to kill him and all of his followers. He had requested the Court to issue restraining orders that prohibited any person of Jewish extraction from traveling near his home. His home on 16th Street N.W. is on the main artery of travel from downtown Washington, D.C., to Silver Spring, Maryland, and the northwest suburbs of Montgomery County that is traversed twice daily in the commute of tens of thousands of civil servants. The Court refused to grant this order. This inaction further infuriated Mr. Khaalis, who now believed the Courts were also involved in this conspiracy.

The U.S. Army provided some information on Mr. Khaalis. His Army service record revealed he was born Ernest Timothy McGee on February 22, 1922, in Gary, Indiana. He was discharged from the U.S. Army in the spring of 1944. Remember, we were preparing to invade Europe in June of that year. I do not think the Army was discharging too many men. However, Mr. McGee was given a "Section Eight" discharge as unfit for military service. In other words, he had some serious mental problems. His brief time in the Army was spent as a member of the Sixth Army band. Other record checks revealed that in 1958 he joined the "Black Moslem" movement in Chicago but broke from them and formed his own sect in Washington, D.C., in 1972. The following year, several members of the "Black Moslem" sect invaded his home on 16th Street N.W. and brutally murdered several members of his family. Those killed included infant children and women.

The MPD and the Chicago and Philadelphia Police Departments were involved in this investigation. The experienced MPD homicide detectives who worked the case said it was the most brutal and bloody crime scene they had ever witnessed. These departments identified the murderers who were tried and convicted for the killings. Washington, D.C., did not then and does not now have the death penalty. They were all sent to federal prison, where most remain.

Telephonic contact was attempted at all three locations. The only successful contact was made at B'nai B'rith with Mr. McGee. The first call was a little disturbing. The phone was answered by a female who said "Ms. Smith of B'nai B'rith, this is the office of Hamaas Abdul Khaalis. Whom shall I say is calling?" This was an unexpected event and called for the immediate identification of Ms. Smith. None of the witnesses reported a female among those who attacked the building. While intelligence on her was being sought, the negotiator identified himself and asked to speak with Mr. Khaalis. Mr. Khaalis was excited but precise in his pronouncements. He immediately went into a long monolog to justify his actions. He insisted that all contacts be made with him because he was in charge. This discussion provided the "Think Tank" with invaluable information on his personality and dictated the direction of all subsequent calls. This is one of the few cases where the initial information was accurate and the subsequent information supported our initial impressions and suggestions to the negotiating team. I think this is because our early information came from reliable sources within the MPD.

Included in his initial ranting were his demands and the justification for them. His insistence on the negotiators understanding his justification also provided a basis for all future contacts and the foundation for intelligence, topics, and tactics. In short, on March 9, 1977, almost four years later, Mr. McGee, now known as Hamaas Abdul

Khaalis, wanted revenge for the deaths of his extended family. His three demands were:

1. Those convicted of these homicides be brought to him for public execution. He thought that a public beheading in Du Pont Circle would be appropriate.
2. The movie "Mohammad Messenger of God" must be removed from theatres in Washington, D.C. It was his view that the showing of the shadow of the actor playing Mohammad was a violation of the Moslem prohibition against a visual depiction of Mohammad. Khaalis extended this to include the shadow of the actor who never appeared on screen. It should be noted that prior to release, this film was viewed by many Islamic clerics who approved all the scenes and the story it told. This made it clear to the negotiating team that Khaalis was an extremist in his religious and probably other views.
3. The fine he paid for contempt of court during the trial of those convicted of killing his family must be returned to him. He thought his ranting during the trial against these killers was appropriate.

Ms. Smith was identified as a young white female of Christian heritage who worked for B'nai B'rith. It was later learned that during the early moments, the leader cornered Ms. Smith who was in fear for her life and determined she was not a Jew. He told her she would work as his secretary and that he would give his life to protect her. In her frightened state, she could not refuse this offer. She did an excellent job as his secretary as she reliably related information to and about him. Some say she is an excellent example of a hostage who is experiencing the Stockholm Syndrome.

As various intelligence agencies and intelligence units within many agencies, bureaus, and departments went to work, the process of negotiations was initiated. Of the three demands, two were easy. The first one was impossible. So the negotiators focused on the last two and said very about the first except to sympathize with Khaalis over the deaths.

Detectives contacted the manager of the one theater showing "Mohammad the Messenger of God." He knew of the siege but did not know the demands. He was happy to help. In addition to his deep sense of public service, the movie was not making any money. Of course, the timing of telling Khaalis of this compliance with one of his demands was another matter. We learned long ago that quick notification of compliance tends to empower the subject and sets the stage for, and expectations of, quick and complete compliance with all demands.

The return of the fine was different and more difficult because the mechanics of the delivery of funds involved the tactical element and literally dozens of tactical and personal options. These included, but were not limited to: Did he want cash? If this was his decision, in what denominations should the money be brought? Who, how, and where should the funds be delivered? Was a direct deposit an option? Should officers deliver the money to him or to his home or bank? As in most cases, the devil is in the details. The negotiators stressed that what Mr. Khaalis was asking was important, so they wanted to get it right. Again, this was rather easily arranged. However, the reporting to him of this arrangement was delayed.

The phone lines to the building were captured so those inside could only speak with the negotiating team. This step was crucial because the news media responded in droves from Capitol Hill some sixteen blocks down Massachusetts Avenue. Because of the activity at the White House with the president and prime minister, the media left on Capitol Hill were suddenly moved from the junior varsity to the starting team with front-page prominence. The media are very competitive, and this sudden and dramatic change in "The Big Story" created a pandemonium of press positioning. More than a few red lights were run as they dashed en-mass up the avenue. The TV folks wanted pictures, the newspaper folks wanted a story, and both wanted interviews. Because of the frequency of "Big Stories" in Washington, D.C., the MPD has a well-thought-out and well-rehearsed press program. Further, all press contacts were with their Public Information Officer. The Chief was in charge and delegated the jobs very well. In addition, and in all fairness, the vast majority of the media in our nation's capital are responsible and mature journalists who understand and play by the rules. Regular media briefings were held. Even when nothing new happened, they were told that nothing new happened. In addition, hundreds of relatives and friends of the hostages and some who thought a relative or friend was a hostage descended on the scene. A local protestant church made its facility available to them. Throughout the siege, relatives came and went. Like the press, they were given regular briefings by the MPD.

I cannot begin to express the professionalism with which the MPD in their handled of this siege. Chief Maurice Cullinane led them. He had an excellent and well-deserved reputation for professionalism and fairness in his dealings with the public, press, and the police he commanded. His career got off to a good start when, as a new parole officer, he was featured, unknown to him at the time, in a Pulitzer Prize-winning photo of him speaking to a three-year-old in the crowd during a parade.

The phone calls that were made day and night went something like:

BB: This is the office of Mr. Hamass Khaalis. Whom shall I say is calling?

N: This is Agent Smith from the FBI. May I speak to Mr. Khaalis?

BB: One moment please. This is Mr. Khaalis.

N. Good afternoon, sir. This is Special Agent Supervisor John Smith from the Federal Bureau of Investigation (now and ever after changed from Agent Smith and FBI).

BB: You listen to me. I am in charge here. There better not be any foolishness on your part or heads will roll, heads will roll. My men will throw Jew heads out the windows. Do not try to come up here. They will all die along with those on the stairs. (Khaalis was very emotional. It was known they controlled the elevators and had filled the stairwells with furniture. Periodically they would pour gasoline down the stairwells from ten-gallon cans. The odor of gasoline was distinct and permeated the building.)

(The tactical team was limited in its use of weapons and approach. They were proficient with the shotgun, but not the rifle. A hostage rescue in this setting required the accuracy of rifle fire, not the scatter effect of shotgun shells. Further, getting onto and then into the top floor of this building presented a challenge. Blowing a hole in the ceiling from the roof was not an option. The gasoline fumes would probably ignite. Getting to the roof was another matter. This tall building stood alone at 1640 Rhode Island Avenue near the corner of Massachusetts and the cross streets around Farragut Circle. The closest building was some distance. All this is by way of saying that a negotiations tactic was the only viable option available to avoid a blood bath of police, hostages and subjects.)

Once Khaalis finished venting, the negotiator said:

> N: I have a list of what you asked us to do. Let me clarify with you what it says. You have some concern with the movie "Mohammad the Messenger of God." (This opened the floodgates of emotional ranting about the Islamic faith and its prohibition against a picture, photo, or any likeness of Mohammad being portrayed. Khaalis went on and on as he educated the negotiator, who asked questions about the tenets of Islam. The negotiator used active listening techniques to encourage Mr. Khaalis who did more than most of the talking. He also said he was interested in learning more about the Hanafi's. Khaalis was appreciative of his interest and spent hours explaining their beliefs as he directed his men to wash their hands and bring him water.)

Later that evening;

> BB: This is the office of Mr. Hamass Khaalis. Whom shall I say is calling?

> Q: This is Agent Smith from the FBI. May I speak to Mr. Khaalis?

> BB: One moment please. This is Mr. Khaalis.

> N: Good evening, Mr. Khaalis, this is Supervisor Special Agent John Smith from the Federal Bureau of Investigation. Do you have a few minutes to review the meals you ordered for tomorrow morning? (I learned at Atascadero that when dealing with a person of the mind- set and mentality of Khaalis, structure, politeness, preciseness, and deference to his "authority" are good rapport-building tactics.)

As I understand it, you want 171 Egg McMuffins along with coffee and orange juice. It is also my understanding that this combination is just about what McDonald's number three breakfast includes. However, it is a mixture of pork and milk products. Based on what you told me earlier, such a mixture may not be appropriate because it violates some of the dietary tenets of Islam. (Do not hold me to the specifics of ham, eggs, milk, orange juice, and such. The point is the negotiator wanted to make sure the order was correct. What Khaalis asked us to do was important. By logical extension, it means he is important. This took time. Later in the day, the lunch menu was an issue because Big Macs, Quarter Pounders with Cheese, along with milk shakes is a similar violation of an Islamic meal tenant. That combination may also be an Orthodox Jewish dietary consideration. However, the negotiators did not discuss Jewish issues. Mr. Khaalis was the focus of this process.)

Later the negotiator called back to see whether it was O.K. for the Hanafis to handle the food or did they needed gloves? If so, how many, what size, and what texture? (Most of this strategy and these ideas came from the think tank. That is their job, and they did it well.)

During the evening and into the early morning hours, periodic telephone calls were made to clarify issues. The negotiators worked in shifts. Khaalis ran the show at all three locations around the clock. He was in charge and made every decision. This activity fit well with the negotiations strategy and the diagnosis and recommendations from the think tank.) Throughout the siege, the friends of relatives of the hostages were housed, in shifts, at the nearby Methodist church where they were regularly briefed. By the third day, Khaalis was worn out. He was still making threats, but with much less emotion. Now came the strategy of arranging an honorable peace treaty that was within the law and would satisfy Khaalis. In short and with the assistance and advice from government psychiatrists, the Metropolitan Police and FBI negotiators effectively dealt with and placated Khaalis. This set the stage for the ambassadors from three Islamic countries, Egypt, Iran, and Pakistan who met with him and built on the rapport the negotiators had developed. These ambassadors were smooth and sincere talkers. I am convinced they could sell an ice-box to an Eskimo. The bottom line is he and his loyal followers surrendered. They were taken into custody.

The hostages were reunited with their families. Because of their number, we could not interview all of them at the same time. Some were immediately reunited, and others were initially interviewed. This proved advantageous. Generally speaking, the Stockholm Syndrome was evident in many of those who were initially interviewed. However, those who spoke with their families first were not as likely to have this reaction to the stress of captivity as were those who were interviewed first. In other words, they were given the opportunity to regain their pre-incident perspective and sense of right and wrong. Of course when dealing with people, one cannot say all or every. However, the basic pattern was evident. Many of the hostages testified for the prosecution during the eight-week trial. Given the personality of Khaalis, we knew well in advance that a plea bargain was out of the question. Khaalis wanted his day in court to further justify his actions to the world press. The press was present en-mass. The Hanafis were all tried and convicted. Their sentences ranged from 24 years to life. The sentence for Khaalis was forty-one to one hundred and twenty-three years. He died twenty-six years into his sentence in the Federal Complex Prison in Butner, South Carolina on November 13, 2003.

Lessons Learned

1. The proper paper work was done well in advance. The law named Posse Comitatus was immediately waived by the president.

2. Most of the lessons learned involved the response to a long-term, multiple sites, and multiple agency response. The need to plan for multiple sites and multiple agency response and responsibilities is a reality that too many departments ignore.

3. These lessons included, but are not limited to, using time to fatigue the subject as the response of law enforcement became more organized, better coordinated, and stronger. We worked fourteen-hour shifts. This approach limited the confusion that usually accompanies the mechanics of shift change.

4. The Stockholm Syndrome took on a new look as we identified predictors and prevention of this mind-set. The predictors were an early statement by the former hostage that included sympathy for the hostage taker or any justification for his actions.

5. Prevention took the form of briefing relatives early, often, and just before they were reunited with their loved one. Thus, they

remained logical and helped bring the former hostage back to reality.

6. The negotiations were recorded and replayed many times in the think tank where a multiple agency effort involved many who would not normally have any involvement in a "local" issue. It is amazing how much is missed the first time around.

7. Mental health experts from several local, state, and federal agencies quickly identified the type of person with whom the negotiators were dealing and in the process made excellent and workable recommendations on how to best deal with him.

8. The demands were softened. The expression "Asked us to do" was used in place of the word demands. Like most hostage takers, Khaalis did not give any thought to the complexity of the demand's details.

9. Our tactical elements learned a lot and changed their approach and training. However, what changes they made lies beyond my expertise. Even if I had the expertise, I do not think tactical innovations and initiatives should be discussed or listed in a public source document.

Let's Be KOOL

The Phoenix, Arizona, Police Department used similar tactics when a night watchman, Billie Joe Guinn, took four hostages in the KOOL television studio just prior to the regularly scheduled evening news broadcast. He entered the studio with a pistol, a plastic bag, and his portable TV set. He may have been mentally ill, but he was not stupid. He brandished his pistol as he took his hostages to and on the sound stage. To demonstrate his determination, he fired a round into the ceiling. That was an attention getter. He wanted his story told on TV during the nightly news program. He arrived a few minutes before it was to be aired.

He claimed to have a bomb in his plastic bag. The reason for bringing his own TV set was to verify that his demands were televised. Mr. Gwinn had heard of others who took over TV studios, made demands, and then surrendered thinking their demands were aired only to later learn they were only aired "in house" on closed circuit, not broadcasted for the general public. So he made an allowance for this possibility and was well prepared. Again, he may have been mentally ill and possibly "off his meds." He was not stupid. He and his four hostages were on the sound stage within minutes of his entering the studio.

The police were quickly called and responded immediately because the TV station shared its parking lot with the Phoenix Police Department. In spite of their rapid response, he and his hostages were already sequestered on the sound stage. One problem was that sound stages have thick glass. This makes them sound proof and also bullet proof. He also claimed to have a bomb. That claim was later found to be false, but it had credibility. Mr. Gwinn was a night watchman at a construction site from which explosives had been stolen. In fact, Mr. Gwinn never touched the explosives and never made a bomb. However, the Phoenix police had to err on the side of caution and operate as if his claim were legitimate. Again, bomb claims get everyone's attention and on many occasions have led to the death of the subject. In this case, the thick glass made an accurate shot difficult, and Mr. Gwinn set no deadlines nor did he verbally threaten anyone. Further, his relatives said he was not a violent person. We all know the best predictor of future behavior is past behavior. His goal was to get his message out because he believed he was a messenger from God and had to warn the world of what he considered the Islamic threat. His goal did not include hurting or killing anyone. Murder would be in violation of the Sixth Commandment. It was logical that a messenger from God would not violate one of God's Commandments. His God-given demands were written on several pages of legal size paper. They included the need for several country western singers to be contacted in an effort to stop the spread of Islam. He "knew" these singers and newsman Dan Rather had been in touch with each other about this threat from the Middle East. Again, Mr. Gwinn was well prepared. So the negotiations process began.

The tactical team was well and quickly positioned. Mr. Gwinn refused to speak on the phone to the negotiating team. However, his primary hostage, Bill Close, was in constant contact with the negotiator. In turn, the negotiator and his team were in regular contact with several of us in Quantico. We became their think tank. We recorded the negotiations so we could listen to them over and over again. We learned long ago that recording this process is paramount. It is amazing how much we miss when we do not record this stressful process.

Our initial strategic plan was to slow things down so we could sort things out. Further, we had learned over the years that giving in to demands too quickly, though it may be expedient, is not generally a good idea because the subject still has enough energy to expand his demands. The stalling tactics typically involve ploys. When a ploy worked, we went with it. When it did not, we moved on. So since we learn while we listen, active listening techniques were used to gather intelligence on Mr. Gwinn and his demands.

I have forgotten how the Phoenix Police Department identified Mr. Gwinn, but they did so very quickly. Intelligence was gathered from his employer. Mr. Gwinn lived alone, but his family was local. They were cooperative and provided excellent and reliable information. They suspected he had not been taking his medication. It might sound like a quick fix would be to give him his meds and he would settle down. The problem is that medication takes time to be effective, and once we begin dealing with medical issues, we must be in contact with the subject's physician or psychiatrist. Just popping a few pills will not usually bring about a satisfactory conclusion. By that I mean the doctor must determine how long he has been "off his meds" before he or she can prescribe the correct dose. Plus, the subject's adrenalin level is typically sky high, and we do not know how much or when he ate or last slept or what other medication he may have ingested. These are some of the issues the medical profession must consider. This takes time.

In this case, his level of preparation was a sign that he was serious and that his demands, as insane as they might sound, were important to him. He was risking his life to broadcast his message from God. So the negotiator prompted Mr. Close to ask questions about the message–how, when, and where it was received. This took time. Mr. Gwinn wanted to read his message. Someone came up with the idea that because he was not licensed to read the news, this could create a problem. Mr. Gwinn took the bait. The negotiator, through Mr. Close, expanded on this problem and its ramifications. He was told that a violation of this law could result in KOOL TV losing its broadcast license. Then, he was told, people would say his message was false because that station was off the air. This peaked his interest. However, he was told that as serious as this problem might seem, there was a solution.

The solution was to contact Mr. Jeffrey Johnson at the Federal Communications Commission to obtain his written approval for this emergency broadcast. It was further explained that a special federal form, FB 124578, had to be signed by Mr. Johnson. Mr. Gwinn understood. As simple as this solution sounded, there was a problem. It was after 5:00 in Phoenix and therefore after 7:00 in Washington, D.C. So, it might take awhile to locate Mr. Johnson. Now traffic problems, accidents, people not going directly home, and all sorts of ploys became available.

In the meantime, the Police Department came up with a copy of federal form FB 124578 and had it signed by the local station manager. The plan was to fax this form to Mr. Johnson for his countersignature. As soon as it was received at KOOL TV from Mr. Johnson, Mr. Gwinn could read his message from God. We did not get into a discussion of God's word and will versus the federal bureaucracy. We did not have to. Mr. Gwinn understood rules and regulations. He was reminded of the displays of licenses he had passed as he entered the studio. He was given regular progress reports on the attempt of the FBI field offices in Washington, D.C., and Alexandria, Virginia, to locate Mr. Johnson. In addition, various police departments in Northern Virginia were included in the search. Further, in the event that Mr. Johnson was not located by any of those searching, two Special Agents of the FBI were waiting for him at his home and had arranged, through the FAA, for a helicopter to fly him back to his office. Again and again, the devil is in the details. However, in this case, your tax dollars were at work resolving these details as quickly as possible.

Of course one can run a ploy for only so long before everyone grows weary. So after a few hours of a futile search for the fictional Mr. Johnson, an alternative plan was concocted. It was decided that perhaps Mr. Close could read the demands. This option was debated at length. On the positive side, Mr. Close had credibility with the Phoenix audience. Mr. Gwinn knew that. That is why he selected KOOL TV over the other TV stations in Phoenix. Once he accepted that arrangement, Mr. Close reminded Mr. Gwinn that as a professional, he had to maintain his credibility. That meant he had to practice the reading. This took time.

Mr. Close read and regularly asked Mr. Gwinn for his input. He then made written notes and comments on the pages as he continued reading and practicing. Once he completed his initial reading and note taking, he read the demands again and again with a normal and professional flow of speech to include the proper emphasis here and there. After several practice sessions, he was ready. He was ready because it was clear that Mr. Gwinn was growing weary. He had been on the sound stage for a few hours for what he considered to be a quick session. We were concerned that his fatigue could turn into frustration, which could result in harming those on the sound stage with him. Once Mr. Close read his message from God and Mr. Gwinn was sufficiently fatigued by the negotiation process, he surrendered. Obviously, he claimed not guilty by reason of insanity. I am told that even today, an officer from the Phoenix Police Department checks with Mr. Gwinn on a regular basis to make certain he stays on his medication. This takes time and requires some resources. However, it takes much less time and requires fewer resources than a siege.

Lessons Learned

1. KOOL TV and most other TV stations around the country have better security.
2. We effectively used time to fatigue and frustrate Mr. Gwinn by surfacing logical issues he had not considered.
3. We worked with him to resolve these issues and offered logical alternatives.
4. We can and did effectively stall for time as we gathered enough intelligence to make our tactic logical and convince Mr. Gwinn it was in his best interest.
5. We relied on the information from his family about his history of nonviolent behavior.
6. Our ploys were logical and made sense.
7. He had no reason to think we were lying because the negotiator was never caught in a lie. He couched his words and suggestions in such a way as to provide some "wiggle room" should he be challenged about a statement. By that I mean he said, "They told me," "I just learned," or "I think federal law."
8. Just as a surgeon uses and needs time for the anesthetic to take effect, so the crisis negotiator needs and takes time to gather intelligence to develop a strategic and tactical plan for dialogue

with a hostage taker to ensure our process is effective and lives are saved (Noesner, 2010).

Bird Seed Bandit

Ever since the late 1960s when a great plan, on paper, to move patients from large mental hospitals to smaller community treatment centers went into effect, we have had a dramatic increase in law enforcement encounters with these patients. The problem is that closing large hospitals was much easier than constructing community treatment centers in neighborhoods that did not want them. That problem continues today largely because mental illnesses are not fatal or curable. So we have many mentally ill people living a normal lifespan outside of mental hospitals who from time to time "go off their meds." Such was the setting in Los Angeles when a mental patient who was a bird lover decided he needed extra money for his flock.

John entered the bank, brandished his weapon, and announced a robbery. Customers and some employees fled while others hid and notified the police and FBI. The response time was quick, and negotiations began almost immediately via a telephone on a desk near where John was standing looking around the bank. The negotiations went something like:

FBI: Hello John. This is the FBI.

John: What is the FBI doing here?

FBI: You are in a federally insured bank. Have you heard of FDIC insurance?

John: I don't need any life insurance.

FBI: Can you hear me O.K.?

John: I can hear you just fine. I am a person without any mental problems. (That was a clue.)

FBI: I can tell that you are very lucid.

John: I don't want anything to drink either. (Another clue.)

FBI: Is everything O.K. with you in there?

John: Everything is fine. Just keep those guys from pointing their guns at me.

FBI: I can take care of that for you. Where do you see people with guns? (Good question. If he can see them, he can shoot them. Further, I have never met a sniper who did not think she or he was invisible. That issue was resolved. However, the manager reported that he could not account for all of his employees and customers.)

FBI: How many people are in there with you?

John: I don't see anyone.

FBI: You don't see anyone?

John: No, but I can walk around and look for people.

FBI: No, you don't have to do that. Just stay where you are so we can talk. (The negotiator did not want John encountering a person hiding under a desk or in the rest room. Such a confrontation could prove fatal. So John stayed at the desk and answered many inane questions.)

John: Is the bank president there?

FBI: No. I think he is playing golf.

John: When will he be back?

FBI: We are trying to get word to him right now.

John: O.K. I will wait until he gets here because I want to talk to someone important.

FBI: I understand that. Important people should talk to each other.

John: O.K. Call me when he gets here. (Other calls were made to keep John at the desk as the tactical team tried to figure out how to best arrest him.)

FBI: I just learned the bank president is on the way. He is in his car, and we have a radio hook up via satellite with him. If you tell me what you want, I can relay your concerns to him on my radio.

John: I have five demands.

FBI: Five demands.

John: God granted me for the journey that there should be no driving for two days.

FBI: No driving.

John: No driving for two days.

FBI: O. K. I got that. No driving for two days.

John: I want everyone in Los Angeles to walk down to the ocean for a cleansing.

FBI: Walk down to the ocean for a cleansing.

John: I want a truckload of birdseed delivered to every bank in Los Angeles.

FBI: One truckload of birdseed to every bank in Los Angeles. What size truck did you have in mind?

John: A big truck.

FBI: O.K. A big truck.

John: I want you to get all this down. It is important. All the trees should be watered by hand.

FBI: Water all of the trees. Is that every tree in the City of Los Angeles or did you have a larger area in mind?

John: I think as many trees as possible.

FBI: O. K. I will see about getting water to a lot of trees.

John: Respect every faith because we are all brothers and the Lord's children.

FBI: Respect for every faith.

John: Number five, everyone will join hand in hand by the ocean.

FBI: Wait a minute. I already have five. Let me repeat what you told me.

So they went over the demands. This took time. During this pro-longed discussion, it was decided to lure John out of the bank for fear that a hostage would suddenly surface, scare him, and perhaps he would shoot. The negotiator then discussed birds with John. It was apparent he had a deep and abiding love for them. So the negotiator told him that some birdseed had been delivered to an area near the bank rear parking lot. In creative detail, he described how the birds were chirping and eating the seeds. He also said they were initially reluctant to eat the seed until everyone with a weapon moved back or holstered their revolver. This was done in such a convincing way that John had to come out to look for himself. The negotiator convinced him to leave his weapon in the bank so as not to frighten the birds. Further, there was more than one door to the bank, so some discussion was held to identify which door John would exit and where he would leave his weapon. All that was accomplished. John came out, saw the birds, and was taken into custody. The FBI secured the crime scene while the bank manager called out to his "missing" employees who, along with several customers, came out of hiding.

Lessons Learned

1. Among the lessons learned was the effectiveness of active listen-ing skills. Although there are several of them, the FBI concen-trated on repeating what John said. This tactic also revealed that John was so focused on his mission of feeding the birds that he lost sight of practical and tactical considerations.
2. The negotiator did an excellent job keeping John calm and in a safe location.
3. He also communicated the scene of hungry birds eating so well that John had to come out and relish in what he had accom-plished. His birds were fed, as was John when he arrived at the county jail.
4. The bank manager was the person who called for his staff to come out of hiding. This is crucial because they recognized his voice. We learned years ago that the use of a person known to and trusted by the hiding hostages was crucial in luring them out of hiding. I recall one case in a school where several students re-mained "missing" after the subject surrendered. After a few attempts by law enforcement officers who walked the corridors

calling their names, it was decided to use a janitor who was known to all of the students. Sure enough, as he walked and called out names, kids came out of wall lockers, from under desks, and from many other places of refuge. When asked why they did not respond to the law enforcement officer, they said they did not recognize his voice and anyone could wander through the school calling names, even this hostage taker.

Amazon Man

This case is discussed here because the subject was in therapy when he engaged in very irrational behavior. After the incident, he was released pending a hearing. He told his therapist that he just snapped under the pressure of too many responsibilities. The crime scene was a jewelry store. During normal business hours, some young girls were in the store to "get their ears pierced" and purchase new earrings. Because of the nature of their business, jewelry stores have several phones around the store on display cases so clerks, while waiting on customers, can answer the phone without leaving valuable merchandise on the counter. This became a factor in this case because on many occasions, hostages, employees, and the subject were on the line at the same time. The problem began when the subject entered the store with a shopping cart from a grocery store and began reaching over the counter to collect watches and other items that he placed in his cart. He was "shopping" for jewelry as one would shop for produce. The store manager recognized this as bizarre behavior and believed he was about to sell more jewelry to one customer than he had sold to many in a month or this person was trying to steal his gems. The "shopper" clarified his intent by brandishing a pistol. The subject continued loading his cart as someone called the police.

One shot was fired. The dispatcher heard it and asked about it. The manager said the guy with the shopping cart just shot the clock. The dispatcher told the manager to tell everyone to get down. The police would be there any moment. At about that time, a negotiator who was in the office came on the line as units responded to the shopping center.

PD: Hi. This is officer Jones with the Sunny Beach Police department.

Sub: This is Amazon, man. (He sounded a little nervous.)

PD: O.K. Amazon Man, can you tell me what's going on?

Sub: (Yelling.) I said my name is Amazon, man not Amazon Man.

PD: I heard you Amazon Man.

SUB: (Yelling louder.) I am Amazon, man. (This exchange was repeated a few times until, and by using a longer pause rather than a comma, the officer understood he was speaking with a person who called himself Amazon, not Amazon Man. It was later learned that he was 5'4").

PD: O.K. Amazon, can you tell me what is going on?

SUB: Yeah. I came in here to get some stuff. I did not know all these strings were attached, man.

PD: Strings attached?

SUB: Yeah. Strings attached. I mean everyone began yelling at me, so to shut them up, I shot the clock, man.

PD: You shot the clock?

SUB: Yeah, man. I shot the clock. (With the receiver covered, the negotiator said "Tell SWAT he shot the clock.")

PD: Did you hit the clock?

SUB: Yeah, man. I shot the clock, and I hit it. That shut them up.

PD: So now they are quiet?

SUB: Yeah, man. That shut them up, and they all laid down. I didn't hit anyone. They just all laid down. Then I went back to work and saw a cop car, about four of them out front in the parking lot. There are cops all over the place out there.

PD: O.K., you can see a lot of officers. (SWAT reported seeing a lone white male in the jewelry store looking into the parking lot. He appeared to have a shopping care in front of him filled with plastic type laundry baskets. No one else was visible.)

SUB: Tell them not to shoot man. I wont shoot at them, and I just put my pistol back in my pocket.

PD: O.K., your pistol is in your pocket.

SUB: Yeah, man. I need both hands to get this stuff into my shopping cart.

PD: What stuff?

SUB: All these watches and shiny stuff like necklaces and rings and stuff. I got to get them into my cart (see Figure 10).

PD: So you are filling the shopping cart with jewelry? Amazon, why don't you just come out and end this quietly.

Figure 10. Laundry baskets with jewelry.

SUB: No way, Jose. I am off to my island. The natives like big shiny stuff.

PD: What natives?

SUB: On the island out in the ocean, man.

PD: Out in the ocean? I think I lost you there. How are you going to get out into the ocean?

SUB: Yeah, man. You guys are gonna give me a 747. Land it right here in this parking lot and take us all to the island.

PD: A 747?

SUB: Yeah, man. A big one.

PD: I don't think that parking lot is big enough for a 747 to land and then take off.

SUB: O.K., then I will need a car, a big car, a limo, to take us to the airport, man.

PD: Slow down. I got to write all this down. (A long discussion followed about the type of car, which airport, what kind of a 747, and which island. By now the five hostages, three young girls and two employees, were listening to negotiations on the extensions. From time to time, they would interject their thoughts.)

GIRLS: We just came in here to get our ears pierced, and now you cops are putting our lives at stake over some lousy jewelry. I'm only seventeen. I don't want to die.

PD: I understand you are scared. We are doing everything we can to end this as quickly and safely as we can.

GIRLS: (Yelling.) All he wants is a damn car. Can't you get him a car and give us our lives back?

PD: We are working as fast as we can.

GIRLS: Well you are not working fast enough. (Shots fired.)

PD: What was that?

MALE: He just shot my filing cabinet.

PD: Your filing cabinet? (He advised SWAT.) Did he hit anyone?

MALE: No. He just hit the metal filing cabinet. Now it has a hole in it.

PD: Can you tell Amazon to pick up the phone?

SUB: I am right here, man.

PD: Amazon, you have got to stop shooting like that. It scares everyone.

SUB: I am not aiming at them man. (At this point, he fired more rounds at the filing cabinet.) Like that, man. I hit what I aim at (see Figure 11).

PD: What did you shoot this time?

SUB: The filing cabinet, man. I am pissed, and shooting makes me feel more relaxed.

PD: I understand that. But that shooting scares them.

SUB: You get me that car, and I will stop shooting.

PD: Amazon. You there?

MALE: No, he is walking around spraying some jewelry cleaner on the walls (see Figure 12).

PD: Can you put Amazon back on the phone?

SUB: What do you want?

PD: Why are you spraying that jewelry cleaner?

SUB: Because if I don't get the car real quick, I am going to put a match to it, and we will all go up in smoke.

MALE: He is back to spraying. Don't worry. That stuff is not flammable. That's why we use it.

PD: Does he know that?

Figure 11. File cabinet with evidence of bullet hits.

MALE: No. He said something like I know that all cleaning stuff burns like gasoline.

SUB: I guess you can see all the stuff I have sprayed around this place. If I don't get what I want, we will all become toast.

PD: You know we are working on getting you what you asked for. It takes time.

SUB: I got all the time in the world.

Figure 12. Glass partition with evidence of cleaning fluid.

Negotiations continued with Amazon, the customers, the male manager, and others who were on and off the phone during the siege. Amazon refused to come out without his hostages until the limo was out front. He said one of the girls would drive to the airport while the police arranged for the 747. The decision was made to park the limo out front and go tactical when they came out. The on-scene commander did not want to risk the lives of the hostages in a vehicle with Amazon. Amazon came out first, crawling behind the shopping cart. He then laid down, shoved the cart away from him, and spread eagled himself on the sidewalk having pushed his pistol ahead of him and well out of reach. SWAT officers arrived and took him into custody. As they were doing so, he said to them, "Tough way to make a livin' aint it." Amazon was taken into custody and released on bond. He visited his therapist one more time. It was learned he had gone off his meds. However, before his court appearance, he left town, never to be heard from again.

Lessons Learned

1. "Off his meds." How many times have we heard that?
2. The dispatcher got the negotiations off to a good start by trying to comfort the hostages as she alerted the crisis response team. Having well-trained dispatchers is crucial. Like any first responder, they can get the process going in the right direction or mess things up so much that it takes forever to get back on track.
3. It is important to listen carefully from the beginning. The mistake made on his name was not serious. During the stress of the opening of negotiations, names are easy to miss.
4. The immediate communication with SWAT about the shots fired was crucial.
5. The negotiator used active listening to draw out Amazon.
6. Because of the many phones in the store, the negotiator never knew who was on which phone. Therefore, he had to err on the side of caution and made the assumption that Amazon was always listening.
7. The negotiator offered Amazon the opportunity to walk out several times. Amazon was still high on adrenaline and not ready to quit. Eventually, he recognized his futility, foolishness, and the potentially fatal situation he had created. He stayed low behind the cover of the limo and shopping cart, pushed the pistol away, and laid there until SWAT took him into custody. I can think of many less dangerous ways to end a siege, but I am not Amazon, man.

The Plot to Kill Nixon

It is not always possible to negotiate with folks who are off their medication or are psychotic. Recall the infamous case of an incident titled "The Plot to Kill Nixon" that is featured in a History Channel documentary (History Channel, 2007). This case involved a bipolar person who tried to hijack an aircraft. In my estimation, negotiating with a bipolar person when they are "up" is like trying to waltz with a whirling dervish. When they are "down," it is like trying to dance with the dead. The good news is the courts have not ordered us to succeed. However, we must make a reasonable effort.

In this case, the subject, Mr. Sam Byke, did not negotiate; he shot and killed people en route to and once on board a Delta Airlines 727 at the Baltimore Washington International Airport. The aircraft was at the gate and in the boarding process when he shot and killed the guard at the screening point and then ran down the jet way to board the nearest aircraft. At gunpoint, he ordered the flight attendant to close the door. As law enforcement was responding from other terminals to the check point and aircraft, Sam shot and killed the pilot, wounded the co-pilot, and then dragged a terrified female passenger from first class into the cockpit and ordered her to fly the plane. While he was occupied in the cockpit, the cabin crew evacuated the aircraft.

The aircraft was attached to the jet way and would have required the removal of the jet way and a tow to the runway. Hence, this attempt was ill thought out, and though Sam spent hours recording his messages, he gave little thought to the mechanics of his venture. Sam was shot and wounded by an Anne Arundle County police officer. He then killed himself. After the incident, his vehicle was located in the airport parking lot. In the trunk was a tape recorder. A few days later his audiotapes arrived via the U.S. mail at three locations that included (a) a Baltimore newspaper reporter; (b) Mr. George Meany of the AFL-CIO in his Washington, D.C., office; and (c) the famed pianist Leonard Bernstein in New York. In Sam's mind, these three people and places were important and connected.

His hours of delusional monologue focused on his plan to achieve world peace by crashing the Delta flight into the White House and in the process killing President Nixon. Do not waste your time here or on site trying to figure out the logic of the discussion and demands of delusional people. Logic may be missing, so listen for the hook. In this case, there were many hooks in his audiotapes. Unfortunately, this whirling dervish never gave anyone the opportunity to discuss his dreams.

Lessons Learned

1. We do not negotiate with an active shooter. Sam was not ready to talk. We should try to ring his phone or get his attention. With Sam in the aircraft behind a closed door, this was not possible.
2. Officer safety and common sense tell us that Sam was not in the right mind-set to talk to anyone.
3. Sam, like many psychotic and emotional people, had planned well up to a point. However, he did not think his plan through. He was destined to fail from the first. Not all situations are negotiable.
4. As Gary Noesner says so well in his book, *Stalling for Time,* do not surrender to the action imperative. Take the time to listen. In that tactic of the negotiations process, you will identify the hook or hooks that in the vast majority of cases will lead to the subject's surrender. A surgeon always waits for the anesthetic to take effect before operating on a patient. So too should crisis negotiators wait until time has had its anesthetic and calming effect on the emotionally driven hostage taker. In this case, time allowed for an effective tactical response.
5. Not all hostage sieges are negotiable. However, once we are on scene, we must try.

References

History Channel. (2007). The Plot to Kill Nixon. A & E Television Networks.
Noesner, G. (2010). *Stalling for time.* New York: Random House.

Chapter 4

THE SAD

Recent research into law enforcement calls to crisis situations collected by the FBI makes it clear that responses to suicidal sieges are increasing across the country. Certainly, one could argue that any person who knowingly decides to confront heavily armed law enforcement officers must be suicidal at some level. Further, anecdotal reports support the increase in the number of suicide calls. This is not to say or suggest that more people are contemplating suicide today than a few years ago. However, it is clear that law enforcement has demonstrated its ability to peacefully resolve many such situations. Therefore, the number of calls to assist with suicidal subjects from doctors, mental health, and the general public has increased and now, anecdotally and according to HOBAS, account for the majority of crisis team responses.

This response has not come without at least one major lesson. In many states, the tactical team no longer intervenes in a solo suicide. They maintain the perimeter, gather intelligence, and perform other duties. This is because in a few cases, they have attempted to save the suicidal person from him or herself. During this attempt, the suicidal person pointed a weapon toward the officers and/or shot at them. To protect themselves, the officers had to shoot the suicidal person. They became involved in a wrongful death lawsuit and lost. There is an old saying that a suicide is a homicide looking for a victim and another that you cannot protect a person from himself. Both of these sayings apply to solo suicides (*Hayes v. San Diego,* 2011).

Ambivalence

When dealing with someone who is suicidal, it is important to remember that we have a subject who is undecided. Psychologists call this a state of ambivalence. If they were totally committed to killing themselves, they would be dead. The unresolved question is, does enough ambivalence exist to sway them into remaining alive . . . if only for today? Remember, as negotiators, it is our job to get people past their immediate crisis, not solve all of their problems. That comes later when they work through their "issues" with a mental health professional.

As I said above, a suicide is a homicide looking for a victim. With that axiom in mind, it is well to remember how potentially dangerous a suicide intervention can be. More and more, departments have initiated the practice of a follow-up contact with subjects. This augments their lessons learned. They discuss the incident with the subject to learn what they said and did that was good as well as what would have been best left unsaid or undone. I have long believed this was an excellent practice for negotiators. It has been my experience that if we do not have a mental health follow-up with suicidal subjects, we are more likely to see them again. You may remember the previous case of the repeat hijacker. The second time around, he improved his procedures and made the situation much more dangerous. Fortunately, only he died.

Personal Pain

The following paragraph is, in my mind, **the most important paragraph of this book**. It is very, very important for the negotiating team to realize, recognize, and remember that when dealing with a suicidal person, we are not necessarily on the same wavelength. Typically, responding teams view suicide as synonymous with a desire to die. The suicidal person is not focused on death. Death is just a path to his or her objective. Their goal is to **escape from pain**. Imagine a pain so great that it surpasses death in the mind of the subject. That means responders should focus on the person's pain not their process. If what I just wrote does not make sense, read it again. The suicidal person wants to **escape the pain** and death is the way of achieving this goal. Therefore, responding teams should focus on doubt that this will work, alternative solutions, or at least delaying their act. They can always try again later if a plan does not work. Dying here and now de prives them of that option. Specific negotiating guidelines are covered at length in the longest chapter of my other book (Strentz, 2012).

Wealth Beyond Measure

Most of us think of suicidal people as down on their luck, broke, in poor health, trying to deal with the death of a person or a relationship, or running from something or someone. There are other causes. One is called bipolar disorder. This disorder was mentioned in Chapter 3 in conjunction with a person who had an antisocial personality disor- der (ASP). In the current case, the subject was only bipolar. Typical of this disorder, there was a family history of similar problems. In addi- tion, he was very wealthy. Because of his many contributions to the community, to include the sheriff's department, the responding depu- ties knew about him.

In the last chapter, I discussed people who were antisocial. This person was the opposite. He was super social. He was a philanthropic member of the community. However, on this afternoon he was prob- ably off his meds. To better understand this negotiation, you should know the policy of law enforcement in this state is not to make a tac- tical entry on a lone suicidal person. The reason is simple. It has been done, and in more than one case, the suicidal person turned the wea- pon away from himself and toward the tactical team that shot and killed him to protect themselves. This resulted in a wrongful death suit that was lost by the responding agency. Because this happened more than once, a policy was written in many departments that no tactical entry would be made in the case of a solo suicide. Certainly such an entry is a noble gesture. However, the lives of the officers are at risk. Should they fire in self-defense, they will be sued and the department will lose (*Hayes v. San Diego,* 2011).

This call about a suicidal barricaded gunman came on at 1235 on a Sunday afternoon. The caller was a relative who said she had reason to believe her cousin was going to drive himself to a local hospital and kill himself there so his organs could be immediately transplanted into the body of a more worthy person. Units responded to the hospital and to his home. He was still at home and was quickly identified. It was learned he was alone in his home in the most expensive section of the county. His estranged wife and their two children were not in the house.

About two weeks prior, the department received a similar call. The two responding deputies were able to talk him out of killing himself. This time he would not speak to them. They observed that he was armed with a holstered automatic pistol. The area was secured by patrol, and a request was made for a response from their negotiating team. Negotiations were conducted from a patrol car with the primary Detective Mike Rand, his secondary Deputy Debbie Eglin, and Sergeant Christina Bavencoff as the scribe working together in a safe location. Their patrol unit provided the opportunity to use the PA if he did not answer his phone. The first call was made at about 1500.

Mike: Afternoon. This is Mike Rand from the Sheriff's Department. Can you tell me what is going on?

Sub: I'm a loser. A terrible father, a worse husband, I am going broke, and I deserve to die. My kids and ex-wives will all be better off without me around, and my organs can do some good.

Mike: That is a pretty negative view of a guy like you who has done so much for so many of us.

Sub: Well, maybe I did it lot for all of you, but I screwed up my personal life, and I have terminal cancer. I will die a slow and painful death soon, so why wait? Dying slowly will waste my organs and could cause them to deteriorate or become infested with cancer and then not be any good for anyone else.

Mike: How do you know you have cancer?

Sub: I just know.

Mike: Did your doctor tell you that?

Sub: He lied to me. He said I didn't have cancer, but I know I do.

Mike: Why do you think your doctor lied?

Sub: That's for him to say. I just know he lied.

Mike: I hear what sounds like ice cubes in a glass.

Sub: You're right. I am drinking rum and Coke. It makes the muscle relaxers taste better.

Mike: How many pills have you taken?

Sub: About six of them.

(At this point the plan was to encourage the drinking so he would pass out or be too weak to pull the trigger. He did become weak.)

Mike: It seems to me that with modern medicine there are several effective treatment programs for cancer.

Sub: Yeah there are, but mine is terminal. I just know it.

Mike: What about your kids?

Sub: My wife has them. That's where they are better off. I have been a terrible parent.

Mike: A terrible parent?

Sub: (He went on and on about things he should have done with his kids. He controlled most of the negotiations. He did most of the talking. Using active listening skills was easy.)

Mike: How old are your kids?

Sub: They are seven and nine.

Mike: That tells me they are young enough for you to make up for any mistakes you may have made.

Sub: They are also young enough to forget what a terrible father I was and recover from my mistakes.

(Note the use of past tense by the subject. Also, time and again, when Mike would try and stress something positive, he came back with a strong negative reply. The negotiations continued for three hours, with the subject doing most of the talking . . . all of which was negative. Attempts were made to convince him to take his medication. He responded that he was a waste of good pills. Ultimately, he thanked the negotiator for talking with him, hung up, and killed himself.)

Lessons Learned

1. Some say that negotiating with a bipolar person who is off his or her medication is like trying to change the color of their eyes by singing "Beautiful, Beautiful Brown Eyes." The point is that their depression is chemically based not reality oriented. We try, but unless they take their medication, our efforts will probably be in vain.

2. Law enforcement officers are accustomed to be being in control. When dealing with this type of person, they tend to retain control. In this case, Mike used active listening in his search for a solution. His skills drew out the subject, who did about 80% of the talking. However, he could not dissuade him from his suicidal intent. We cannot save a person from himself.

3. In my many years of dealing with negotiators and negotiations, it has become clear to me that when we lose negotiators, when they leave the team, it is usually after an unsuccessful attempt to negotiate with a suicidal person. All too often, we blame ourselves rather than accept the fact that some situations are beyond our control. That is why a Post Critical Incident Debrief is so important. In this case, Mike had the support of his partner, his team, and his department.

4. As Mike said of his partner to me in an email and in their presentation at the California Association of Hostage Negotiators Annual Training Conference, no matter how hard we try, some people have already decided to die. All we accomplish is delaying the inevitable. I think Mike is right. However, we do not know until the end if their decision was the inevitable or if we can change their minds. The courts have told us to always make a reasonable effort. We have ordered ourselves to always succeed. That is a noble mind-set and goal, but it is not always realistic.

5. It is important for us to take care of our team members. We must remain alert to their stress and pick up on their messages that "things are not right." Even if we are wrong in our assessment, it does not hurt to ask. In this case, Debbie's husband is also a law enforcement officer who had experienced a stressful situation. She recognized symptoms in Mike and encouraged him to talk them out. He did and in so doing has helped many negotiators

recognize similar symptoms and deal with rather than bury them.

Jane the Jumper

A few weeks later, the same sheriff's department and the same primary and secondary negotiators were called around noon by a motorist saying a female was standing on the barrier in the center of an overpass on the highway side of the chain link fence. She was leaning forward but holding onto the fence. It looked to him like she was going to jump (see Figures 13 and 14).

The response was immediate. Traffic on the highway under the bridge was stopped and re-routed as negotiators and other units responded (see Figure 15).

The person on the bridge was in her thirties and unarmed. She alternated her hold on the chain link from one hand to the other as she leaned forward and then pulled herself back. It was cool and very windy. Patrol officers recognized her as a "local homeless person"

Figure 13. The subject talking to the team.

Figure 14. The negotiating team of San Diego Sheriff Deputy Debbie Eglin, Detective Mike Rand, and Sgt. Russ Moore wearing the baseball hat. Russ found a crate as a prop so the negotiators could make eye contact.

whom they believed was living under the bridge. She was known to be addicted to meth. It was also known that she had lost custody of her children, who were in foster care.

Face-to-face negotiations were initiated using a male and female team with a sergeant as the team leader. He located some boxes so the negotiators were on her level and could make eye contact. It was noticed that when the negotiators approached her, she moved away. This tactic was used throughout the process. The negotiators gradually moved her from the center of the overpass toward one end where the drop was less. Other responding units were moved away from the end of the overpass toward which she was being moved (see Figure 16.) The plan was to continue this movement. The negotiations and her movement continued for almost three hours until she slipped at 1544 and fell to her death.

Because Deputy Debbie Eglin and Detective Mike Rand both negotiated, I will refer to their efforts as "Nego" rather than jump back and forth between them.

Figure 15. Notice the school bus. Imagine the problems these kids could create.

Nego: Good morning, mam. I am Deputy Eglin with the San Diego County Sheriff's office. The deputy with me is Mike. What can I call you? .

Jumper: Nothing. Just go away.

Nego: Well, we cannot just go away. That would be against the law.

Jumper: Then leave me alone.

Nego: Alone?

Jumper: Yeah, just stay away and leave me alone.

Nego: Can you tell me what brought you here this afternoon?

Jumper: I walked.

Nego: Do you live near here?

Jumper: Yeah.

Figure 16. The subject started in the center. After two hours she was almost over the grass.

Nego: What I meant was why are you here in such a dangerous place?

Jumper: Because I want to die.

Nego: You want to die?

Jumper: Yeah, just end it all here and now.

Nego: Ending it here and now is a serious decision. Why here and why now?

Jumper: My life is shit.

Nego: Shit?

Jumper: Yeah, just plain shit. My kids are gone and my boyfriend is cheating on me. He lives right up there in that house.

Nego: Where are your kids?

Jumper: The county has them.

Nego: You mean they are in a foster home?

Jumper: Yeah. The court put them there.

Nego: The court put them there, the court can also give them back.

Jumper: That ain't gonna happen.

Nego: Why not?

Jumper: Because I use meth.

Nego: O.K. you use meth. A lot of people have used meth and quit. You can quit too.

Jumper: No. I tried. I can't quit. I am just plain shit. No good for anyone.

Nego: You are certainly good in your kids' eyes.

Jumper: No. They county has them, and they are better off without me.

Nego: What about your boyfriend?

Jumper: That's a joke. He is cheating on me. He don't need me. I am just taking up space.

Nego: How do you know he is cheating?

Jumper: Someone told me. That is why I came up here. I want to confront him.

Nego: Talking to him is a good idea.

Jumper: Yeah. But he ain't home.

Nego: We can send people to get him. Do you know where he is?

Jumper: No.

Nego: Then why not wait until he comes home or you have some idea where we can find him?

(During this protracted discussion, it was noticed that when some-one approached from one direction, she moved away. Therefore, the team leader, Sergeant Russ Moore, set up people to arrive from one direction, and, as the photo demonstrates, she moved a step at a time toward a place where a leap or fall would not be fatal. Un-fortunately, she lost her grip before she was in a safe area. She slipped, fell, and died.)

Lessons Learned

1. The most dramatic and tragic lesson learned again is that we cannot save a person from him- or herself. In this case, Jane placed herself in a dangerous position and situation on that ledge of that bridge and, in so doing, lost control of her fate.
2. People spend years making a wreck of their lives. Negotiators cannot expect to turn these years of turmoil around in one siege or session. We focus on delay, alternatives, and doubt as we offer help and search for the "hook." In this case, the usual hook of her children did not seem to work. It appeared that her boy-friend might be a hook. Unfortunately, she fell before he was found.

Another Jumper

When George Allen was the head coach of the Washington Red-skins, he often used the phrase, "It isn't over until the fat lady sings." With this expression, he motivated his teams to keep playing to win until the last whistle blew. This case is a good example of how impor-tant it is to remember that expression when dealing with suicidal sub-jects after they are in custody.

At 1900, the San Diego County Sheriff's Department received a call from a motorist who reported a white male standing on the railing of IH8 Pine Valley Bridge. This bridge stands some 250 feet above the valley and is the site of some three-dozen suicides each year (see Fig-ure 17). Therefore, the department has deputies living in and assigned to that part of the county. The first responder was quickly on scene. He calmed the subject, diverted traffic and did a dozen things to set the stage for the negotiations process including calling for a negotiator. He also ran the tag of the car parked near the jumper (see Figure 18). It

Figure 17. It's a long way down.

came back to Terry Hall. There were no wants, warrants, or any previous law enforcement contacts. A negotiator, Sgt. Russ Moore, was quickly on scene.

Russ: Hi. My name is Russ from the Sheriff's office. What can I call you?

Jumper: My name is Terry, and I came here to die.

Russ: Can you tell me why?

Terry: I killed my wife.

Russ: You killed your wife?

Terry: Yeah. Her body is in the car.

Russ: In the car parked over there?

Terry: Yeah. She is in the back seat.

Figure 18. The subject's car contained the exhumed body of his wife.

Russ: What led up to her death?

Terry: She was cheating on me. The Navy sent me back from my deployment to get things straightened out. We argued and I lost it. Now I have to die.

Russ: Why do you have to die?

Terry: Because I killed her.

Russ: It sounds to me like there is a lot more to the story. If the Navy thought your situation was serious enough to send you home, I think they had a good reason.

Terry: Yeah. I heard from friends that she was cheating with guys here in San Diego. I told my Chief. The Navy would not send me back, so I hurt myself to force them to send me back here to get things squared away. I confronted her. We argued. Got into a fight and I killed her. Then I buried her and tried to hang myself, but the tree limbs kept breaking. So I dug her up, washed her, put on her pajamas, placed her in the car, and came here.

(Do not try to introduce logic into this exchange and situation. He was very emotional. By definition, emotional people tend to lose their logic.)

Russ: Wow. You just covered a lot of stuff in a short time. Right off you told me there was a good reason for you to come home. You tried to talk to her. She started a fight and then she died. It sounds to me like you could make a case for self-defense. Under the law, there is a big difference between killing someone and self-defense. Have you ever been arrested?

Terry: No, sir. I couldn't join the Navy if I had a record. I don't have any traffic tickets either.

Russ: That will work in your favor. You were serving your country in a dangerous place, and you have no record. Not even a traffic ticket. You were honorably serving your country, and she dishonored you be cheating on you. That just isn't right.

Terry: Yes, sir. My plan was to make a career of the Navy.

Russ: Tell me about what you did in the Navy.

(He then went into a long story that began with Boot Camp and ended with his deployment. It was clear he took a great deal of pride in his service and was respectful of the authority of Russ. Note, he began calling him sir. It was clear that he did not have any experience with the criminal justice system, the alternatives and limitations involved within the system. Because he injured himself so severely, he had violated the Uniform Code of Military Justice and was facing a less than honorable discharge. However, in his mind, none of his problems was his fault. His wife, whom he met in a Tijuana Bar, had caused these problems by her promiscuous behavior. So, it was all her fault, plus the Navy was to blame for not listening to him and sending him home to get his life squared away. He wanted to make a career of the Navy, but her behavior and the Naavy's lack of concern robbed him of his future.)

Russ: Wow. You did a lot, and then she caused the problem. (Encouraging projection, blaming the victim, often works during an interview. It also works during negotiations. Remember, Terry was ambivalent, so Russ built on that. He found some hooks: his pride in his service, the possibility of self-defense, and his sorrow. Plus, Terry knew little about the system.)

Terry: Yeah, she sure did cause it from beginning to end. I lost it. I wanted to give her a decent burial. Then, I just could not live with myself after what I did so I wanted to end it all. (Notice the use of past tense. He wanted to end it all, not I am going to end it all.)

Russ: Yeah, I can tell. Why don't you come down off that ledge so we can talk?

Terry: Yes, sir. You're right. There's no point in losing my life over what they did to me. You are right. This is not going to prove or solve anything. Can I call her mother?

Russ: No problem. Just as soon as you come down and get into the car, you can make that call.

Terry: Okay, here I come.

Terry surrendered at around 2200. He offered to drive his car with the exhumed body of his wife in the back seat to the station. He was told that was against the law. A deputy would take care of that. Terry got into the patrol car and was driven to the station. However, it was not over. A few days later, during the investigation by the police into his homicide, he was disarmingly helpful. This became evident when during a trip in a police car, he reached over the seat and grabbed the pistol from the detective. There was a fight. Some shots were fired. The detective won. Terry said he wanted to kill himself with the pistol. So, it isn't over until it's over. Terry went to trial. He pled not guilty and was sentenced to 24 years in prison.

Lessons Learned

1. Active listening helped surface the hooks of his pride in his service and his projection onto his wife for all their problems. The negotiator gave Terry the chance to tell his side of the story. As Terry talked, he identified several hooks.
2. These hooks were used to draw him out.

3. Again, he was ambivalent. If he had been totally committed to dying, he would have jumped well before the negotiator arrived. In this case, there was enough indecision to draw him out and down from the ledge. That isn't always the case.

4. Russ used many of the recommended guidelines for negotiating with this type of person. Many of them are set forth in *Psychological Aspects of Crisis Negotiations* and *Crisis Negotiations*. I mention this to him. His comment was, "Of course I did. That is good stuff that works." Or words to that effect.

5. It isn't over until it is over. Terry's attempt to kill himself in the patrol car is a reminder that suicidal people are emotionally unstable and must be protected from injuring others or themselves.

Valley Volley Ball

Early one weekday morning, the police received a call from Joe Jamison, the principal of the local high school, who said he wanted to report a coach who had molested two female students. He said he fired the coach, dismissed him on the spot, and then remembered the coach had broken the law. Two officers from juvenile division were advised. They said their ETA at the school would be about an hour. Given the distance and time involved, they advised the principal to isolate the victims from each other and other students until the responding officers could interview them. The principal said he would remove them from their classes and keep them in his office. A few minutes later, the police received a call from an elderly lady who said her neighbor had just driven into his driveway and side swiped her car in the process. She knocked on his door and heard him yell at her to go away. She said he was a very nice person who taught at the local high school and was always pleasant to her. She asked the police to conduct a welfare check. A patrol officer was dispatched.

When the patrol officer arrived, he knocked on the neighbor's door to confirm her call, complaint and concern. He saw her damaged vehicle. He then heard a shot fired from inside the house next door, took cover, and called for a backup. No other shots were fired. He asked dispatch to call the residence. Dispatch did, a male answered the phone and said the officer should get back in his police car and go away because everyone in the house was going to die. Dispatch engaged him in conversation. Negotiators were notified, and a tactical callout was issued.

A negotiations team was assembled, and a call was made from their office. The residence was identified as the home of the coach about whom the principal had complained. The first responding offi cer reported the full names of the people in the house, which he had obtained from the neighbor. A quick check revealed no prior calls to that residence and no history of criminal activity or traffic stops. In addition, the owner of the home, Tom Smith, had a CCW. He owned and had registered a 9 mm Sig Sauer. He was employed as a high school coach. From neighbors it was learned that his wife Kathleen, age 32, was a teacher who had taken leave to care for their two young children, ages 2 and 5. In addition, her parents and his were retired school-teachers who lived in a nearby town.

The negotiator (N) made a call to the house. Tom (TS) answered.

N: Good morning. This is Kim Jefferson. I am with the Smalltown Police Department. Can you tell me what is going on this morning?

TS: It's none of your business. Just go away. This is all very personal and will soon be history.

N: Be history?

TS: I don't want to talk to you or anyone. I just want to end this mess before it affects my whole family.

N: Well, we can't just go away. The law says we must clear the call. That means talking to you about this morning.

TS: This morning was a teacher's worst nightmare.

N: Worst nightmare?

TS: Yeah. Two kids accused me of fondling them. It's two against one. My career, my life, is over.

N: Why is it over?

TS: I will never work with kids again. Kathleen will not be rehired, and our kids will bear the brunt of these accusations. It's two against one. There is only one way out for all of us.

N: Tom, are you thinking about killing yourself? (This is the difficult but necessary question. According to mental health professionals, this question will not trigger a suicidal attempt.)

TS: That is the easy part. It is Kathleen and the kids who are the issue.

N: What issue?

TS: The accusations against me will affect them, so they have to go with me. With me gone, Kathleen will not be able to support everyone and will bear the brunt of the accusations. My life insurance will not pay off. Killing myself is easy and necessary. I just cannot bring myself to kill them.

N: I appreciate your honesty. Let's just take awhile to talk about this. (Good idea. Buy time. Slow things down and listen for the hook.) You are getting way ahead of me. Tell me about this morning.

TS: Isn't that why you are here, to arrest me? I am accused of child molestation. Do you know what a serious charge that is?

N: Let's slow down. Yes, child molestation is a serious accusation. Proof is another matter. I did not know anything about any accusations of child molestation. Officers are out front because your neighbor was worried. In her words, she heard a shot ring out.

TS: Well, after you get the word, you will arrest me.

N: Again, you are getting ahead of me. Let's take this one step at a time. Begin by telling me about this morning.

(The negotiator, an experienced law enforcement officer, believes that Tom, like Terry in the previous case, knew little about the criminal justice system, much less investigative procedures. She is using ALS to draw Tom out to tell his story. She is taking time to get the subject's version of events; his view of reality is vital. We must understand, not approve or agree with, what he says or has done. She has lived in Smalltown since childhood and attended the high school at which Tom is a coach. She knows the story of how he turned their girls' volleyball team into state champions. Intel from the department has provided some sketchy information on the call from the high school. Two juvenile officers are responding. It is clear that Tom is so focused on his situation at school that he does not understand the big picture. We have heard of tunnel vision in shootings. In this case, and typically in all cases of high stress, the person under stress has tunnel vision. In addition, the negotiator is trying to get Tom to focus on one thing at a time. He has a full plate. She wants him to step back, "Go to the Balcony," and try to be more open to events and reality. She knows she should not tell Tom to relax. That will not work. If he could relax, he would not be out of touch with reality. Instead, she is giving him some direction and focus, so in the process he can begin to relax. People under stress often respond to logical suggestions. They are seeking relief. Even if the suggestion does not work, it conveys concern. An important mind-set to assume is that you are dealing with a victim. As law enforcement and correctional officers, we treat subjects differently than victims. Here we have a subject who may be a victim.)

(Tom told her about the accusations of molestation by two girls on the volleyball team. He said was fired by the principal. He said he tried to explain to the principal that he told them they would not be going to the first away playoff games because conference rules limited the number of players he could take. However, as they advanced in the playoffs, the number of players allowed would increase, and then they would take their place on the team. He made that decision because they were the youngest. He wanted to give the seniors the chance to play as much as possible. He was convinced that they would easily win the first series of away games. However, both girls stormed out of his office in tears before he could get beyond telling them about the decision on the first game lineup. He then went on to say that teaching and coaching were his life and, without them, well, it was all over. He had decided that to save his wife and kids the embarrassment, he would "Take them with him.")

(Kim clarified his story, by saying "Tell me about the meeting in your office." Tom said he told the two girls at the same time because he knew they were friends. He did not want to tell one and have the other learn of it before he had a chance to speak with her. Plan A was to tell them when his assistant coach Georgia Johnson was present. However, the two arrived early. Georgia was still with a class, so he told them in her absence.)

N: So you told them together, and they left your office?

TS: Yes, together.

N: Where is your office?

TS: My office is next to the equipment room. Jim was there. He heard them slam my door on their way out and came over to see what was happening.

N: Did he hear them knock on your door?

TS: My door is always open. It's a rule. I never close my office door. They did when they left.

(The negotiator is wearing two hats. She is the negotiator, but she is also a cop trying to get the subject's version of events and hopefully the facts or at least the sequence of events. Of course, she needs his version to negotiate. She is also clarifying issues and gaining some insight into Tom's knowledge of the law and how investigations are conducted. We learn when we listen. Tom is not in custody, so Miranda warnings are not an issue. On the positive side, it does not seem logical that a person would molest two girls at the same time in an office with the door open that is next to an occupied equipment room. Something isn't right.)

N: O.K. just talk me through the sequence of events. Did they walk into your office together?

TS: They were together and all smiles. That changed when I told them what coach Johnson and I decided we had to do. But before I could fully explain our reasons or rationale, much less the next series of games, they left my office in tears and slammed the door behind them. The next thing I knew, Mr. Jameson was in my office accusing me of molesting them and ordered me out of the building.

N: He ordered you out of the building?

TS: Yes, he did. I drove home. I guess I drove into the driveway too fast. I think I hit Mrs. Johansen's car. I told Kathleen what happened. She was stunned. The kids began to cry. She tried to console them. I went upstairs to our bedroom and got my gun. I don't know what happened, but it went off. That really got the kids and Kathleen crying.

N: The gun went off?

TS: Yes. I was upstairs, and the round went into the ceiling.

N: Was anyone hurt?

TS: No.

N: Where is the gun now?

TS: I have it in my lap.

N: Is it cocked?

TS: No.

N: That's good to hear. Accidental discharges occur a lot. The ceiling of our locker room is proof of that.

TS: You mean cops have guns go off accidentally?

N: More often than we care to admit.

TS: I hate to say that is good to hear. But now I don't feel so stupid.

N: I think stress, not stupidity, is the cause.

TS: I guess I am under a lot of stress.

N: I think you are. I also think you may be in less trouble than you think. (Hope)

TS: Less trouble?

N: Yes, much less trouble.

TS: What do you mean? I lost my job and my career, and I am on the verge of ending it for all of us.

N: Did you molest the girls at school?

TS: No.

N: I believe you.

TS: But it is two against one.

N: Not really.

TS: What do you mean not really? (Now who is using ALS?)

N: Do you have any idea how many false allegations of sexual assault, molestation, rape, and on and on we work each week? You know, you should talk to an attorney. A lawyer can tell you more about this sort of thing than I can.

(We have just turned a corner. The negotiator is creating some doubt about the story told by the girls, created delay on his part, and is offering help and hope. The use of an attorney can be considered an alternative to the use of a pistol. She is focusing on DAD–doubt, alternatives, and delay. In this case, doubt is not about his method but doubt about the validity and legality of the allegations. It is not our job to solve the problems of suicidal people. However, when logical alternatives occur and, as in this case, it looks like the subject is off base in his assessment of the situation, we should offer suggestions and clarify the situation. Even if the suggestions are wrong, they communicate care. Suicidal people feel alone in their grief. This helps break through that barrier of loneliness.)

It is clear that Tom has no idea how investigators work or how investigations are conducted. He has no idea how many people lie to law enforcement and correctional officers. He is a good coach, but when it comes to law enforcement issues and procedures, he was naive. The story has a happy ending. The juvenile officers interviewed Jim and Coach Johnson, who said, among other things, that she told Tom not to talk to those two alone. They are the least mature girls on the team and probably the poorest players as well. Coach Johnson said there was no way that Tom molested those two scatter brains. Jim agreed with Coach Johnson and confirmed the office door was open. With this background, they interviewed the two young girls separately. Using standard techniques, both girls admitted that nothing happened. They were expelled. The principal apologized for "Going off half cocked." The team went on to win another state championship. There are those who say the girls played their hearts out to prove to the world that Coach Tom was a good coach and not a pedophile. Be that as it may. This story has two happy endings. The other is no suicide. The negotiations process took time and once again worked.

Lessons Learned

1. Take time to allow the subject to tell the sequence of events while other officers are gathering the facts. As the subject talks, the negotiating team begins to gain insight into the situation and starts to identify "hooks."
2. With suicidal people, the acronym of DAD works for me.
   a. Delay; you can always kill yourself tomorrow. If you do it today, you lose that option.
   b. Alternatives involve the discussion of other solutions.
   c. Doubt focuses on the fact that this course of action is one from which there may be no turning back.
3. In this process, we have two things we try to identify. They are **hooks and hot buttons**.
   a. A hook is something we can use to get the subject out.
   b. A hot button is a topic we want to avoid. Both should be identified and written on the situation board for all to see and remember.
4. Time was also used to evaluate the subject, who, though intelligent, had no idea how the investigative process works. This lack of knowledge was used to induce doubt. In other words, this was not an open and shut matter as he feared. Investigators would get to the truth.

It is not the purpose of this text to review all the tactics and techniques of the negotiations process. The purpose here is to provide examples of what works and on occasion, what does not.

Sample Negotiation Position Paper

NPP 2 (This is the second report.)

Date

Time 1045 AM

Status

1. The subject remains in his private residence he entered two hours ago. He believes he was fired from his position as a girl's volleyball coach at Smalltown High School. Accusations that he simultaneously molested two female students in his office are now being investigated at the school. He has a 9 mm Sig Sauer that is registered to him.
2. The subject is keeping police at bay by holding his two children (ages 2 and 5) and his wife Kathleen (age 32) as his hostages. He is threatening homicide and suicide. He is in the kitchen downstairs. His wife and their two children are in an upstairs bedroom.
3. The subject is despondent and has admitted considering suicide.
4. The subject's telephone line has been captured.

Assessment

1. This is a hostage siege with the possibility of homicide and suicide.
2. The subject does not have a criminal record and there is no history of calls to his residence.
3. The subject is despondent over accusations. He is naive and unaware of police investigative procedures.
4. The subject is intelligent.
5. The subject is not proficient in the use of firearms.
6. The subject is ambivalent but communicative and confused.

Recommendations

1. The crisis negotiations team should focus on stalling for time by keeping the subject occupied on the phone while the investigation at the high school is conducted.
2. The tactical team should maintain a low profile.
3. The crisis negotiations team should encourage the subject to talk about his success as a coach.
4. Any additional recommendations are dependent on the findings of the investigators at the high school.

Tell Aunt Nini Good-bye

Another case involved a young girl who went away to college. She was in a new setting far from home. She was smart, attractive, and athletic. She was at a state university on a baseball scholarship. Although she was doing well in class, her personal life was not going well. She thought she found the love of her life, only to discover that he was more involved with another girl. She became despondent and her grades suffered, as did her athletic ability. She withdrew from her on-campus church group and was late for most of her classes. All this came to light at around 9:00 a.m. when she was seen on the roof of her ten-story dorm walking around in her pajamas. When her dorm adviser tried to talk to her, she threatened to jump. It was obvious that she was not armed. There was no suicide note in her room. She had missed breakfast and her first class. The campus police were called.

There was a memo of understanding (MoU) among the campus police, city police, county sheriff, and state police regarding incidents on campus. The negotiators from each department belonged to the same state negotiators organization. In addition, they had trained together. The bottom line is they knew each other, as did members of each department's tactical team. The multi-agency call out followed the MoU.

It was decided to use a female negotiator with a male backup in a face-to-face discussion. The primary negotiator stuck her head out from a crack in the roof access trap door. She spoke from that vantage point until she thought it safe to ask the subject, Stacey, if it was O.K. for her to come out onto the roof. What they had going for them was the fact that Stacey was walking around where people could see her at a time when many students were in the courtyard. She was not close to the edge where she might slip and fall off the roof. This suggested that she was ambivalent and perhaps undecided enough to listen to reason. In addition, students in the dorm knew her and provided the officers with a lot of information on Stacey that included her situation with her boy friend as well as her strengths.

The negotiator's first goal was to engage Stacey in conversation to establish her concern for Stacey and help her talk about her situation. The negotiations went something like:

N: Hi, Stacey. My name is Janet. I am with the Alma Police Department. I would like to talk to you.

Stacey: I really don't want to talk to anyone. Just leave me alone.

N: I understand what you are saying, but leaving you alone right now is not an option.

Stacey: Why not?

N: Well, the law says we cannot walk away from a situation like this.

Stacey: That is a stupid law.

N: Well, there are a lot of laws I do not agree with, but the law is the law.

(The negotiator was speaking through a partially open door. She asked Stacey if it was O.K. for her to come out onto the roof. Stacey said O.K. as she backed away from the door but not toward the edge of the roof. When the negotiator came onto the roof, she sat down on the ground as her male secondary appeared at the door. Stacey asked who he was. The negotiator told her he was there to help her, relay messages, and get things for her. Stacey smiled a little and said, "So he is working for you?")

N: Well, we are a team. We work together.

Stacey: But you are in charge. (Evidence of her hostility toward men?)

N: Right now I am in charge of talking to you, and Ed is here to help. (Before she introduced Ed, she made sure that the name of Stacey's former boyfriend was not Ed.)

Stacey: I don't feel like talking to you with him listening.

N: Why not?

Stacey: I don't think men understand what they do to women. (Hostility or reality?)

N: That may be true of some men. I have known Ed for a long time, and he is very understanding.

Stacey: A man who understands. That is an oxymoron. (Stacey is no dummy.)

N: An oxymoron. I don't think anyone ever called Ed an oxymoron before now. (Stacey did not smile, so Janet moved on.) Can you tell me what is going on?

Stacey: There is just too much going on to talk about it.

N: Well, pick a part of it, and we will go from there. (Janet is trying to get Stacey to compartmentalize her stressors and take on one at a time.)

Stacey: Well, I am going to flunk out of school.

N: Flunk out?

Stacey: Yes. My grades are going down the toilet, and I am headed in the same direction.

N: The same direction?

Stacey: Yes. (Sarcastically.) My brilliant academic career is over.

N: Who told you that?

Stacey: No one had to tell me. I know when I am flunking out.

N: Let's come back to that later. Is it O.K. with you if we check that out?

Stacey: Go ahead. I don't care. (Their conversation was being recorded and relayed to other negotiators in the think tank who were checking out things said by Stacey. This is an intelligence function that is best performed by trained negotiators. They know what needs follow-up. In this case, they began checking her status in her classes to verify her fears. It turned out, she had failed some tests. But it was early enough in the semester to make up some of the lost points. She would not get an A in those classes, but she was far from failing. This is good information, but not the right time to tell Stacey.)

N: So your grades are a problem?

Stacey: That's right, and without good grades, I cannot play ball, so I will lose my scholarship and have to return home as a failure.

N: I understand the need to maintain good grades. What academic level must you maintain? A 3.5, a 3.0, or what?

Stacey: A 2.0.

N: You sound more intelligent than a 2.0 to me. I would peg you at close to a 4.0.

Stacey: I was a 3.9 in high school. That is how I got here. But that is ancient history.

N: Ancient history?

Stacey: Yep. It is what I do here that counts, not what I did back home. (It was noticed that although Stacey paced when she talked, her walking did not bring her close to the edge. She generally stayed about ten feet from the edge.)

N: Where is back home? (This got Stacey talking about her high school academic and athletic accomplishments. Those were the good days of her life. She spoke of them with pride. It appeared that a hook had been identified.)

Stacey: But that is all over.

N: It is only all over if you want it to be all over. You are the same person in a different place. Are you thinking about killing yourself?

Stacey: (A long delay.) I guess that is why I came up here.

N: Let's just talk for a while about what is going on. You said this place is different.

Stacey: That is the problem. This place is too different.

N: Too different.

Stacey: Yes, just too different. I do not have my Nini to talk to. (Who is Nini? Find out fast.)

N: Nini? Who is Nini? (This opened the floodgates of tears about her aunt, who raised her after her parents were killed in an auto accident. Nini was her rock. Officers in her hometown who were gathering intelligence for those on campus verified this. These officers were also negotiators. Thus, they knew the questions to ask and what answers were important. Unknown to Janet at the time, they put Nini in a squad car and came code three to the scene. It was obvious from the smile on Janet's face that she recognized the hook. Now the question was where, when, and how to use it? Ed also recognized it and communicated this to Janet. That is one responsibility of the secondary negotiator.)

Stacey: Why are you smiling?

N: Oh, I was just thinking about my favorite Aunt Babe. Her real name was Josephine, but everyone called her Babe. Like your Nini, she was a gem. (It is not a good idea to lie to a person with whom you are negotiating. However, in this case, it was only half a lie. The negotiator was smiling for two reasons: One was identifying the hook, and the other was her favorite aunt Babe. She now had some common ground with Stacey.)

(Time passed with more discussion about life back home versus life on campus and the importance of Aunt Nini in her life.)

Stacey: Will you tell Nini that I am sorry I failed her and that it had to end this way? (This was the golden moment for Janet. Now to use the hook.)

N: O.K. But think for a moment. (She took a brief pause for effect.) How would you feel if a police officer came to your dorm and told you that she had a message for you from your Nini who had just killed herself? (Janet said police officer rather than I because she wanted Stacey to feel the full effect of being given this terrible news by a total stranger. We never practiced that. Janet was a natural.)

That did it. Stacey began crying uncontrollably and fell to her knees. Janet and Ed rushed to pick her up as she sobbed in Janet's arms. It was over. They took her from the roof back to her room. Janet stayed with her until Nini arrived. Stacey stayed in school and on the team, which did very well making it to the nationals twice before she graduated. She took a job coaching at a local high school. She was an attractive girl, so I assume she did well socially.

Lessons Learned

1. It is important to listen to the subject who is drawn out to talk by the use of ALS. With suicidal subjects, it is important to remember that if they were 100% sure they wanted to die, they would be dead.
2. The key is to determine whether there is enough ambivalence to change their mind. We can do this by letting them talk as our team listens for the hooks and hot buttons.
3. The importance of gathering and verifying intelligence cannot be overstated. We must clearly identify what we know, what we think we know, what we need to know, and what we do not know. This information should be on the situation board for all to see. This is one of the problems when going face to face. There is no situation board to remind the negotiator of hooks and hot buttons. Some negotiators who go face to face have a code with their secondary. It can be as simple as one cough for hook and two for hot button. It is much easier if the primary has an earpiece and practices the passing of information with the secondary. This is more complex than passing notes back and forth, so practice is necessary.
4. Obviously the negotiator developed a relationship. Having a favorite aunt of her own augmented her demeanor.
5. The importance of Mutual Aid Pacts and Memos of Understanding is obvious.
6. The selection of a female negotiator was logical, and a male backup, whose name was different from the boyfriend, was important. Along these lines, the male secondary or backup negotiator played well with the subject.
7. Time was taken to allow Stacey to tell her story. In the telling, hooks were identified. The most important hook was her aunt.
8. Intelligence gathered by the think tank was communicated to the field, where experienced officers understood what they were

after and then, once locating the aunt, transported her to the site immediately.

9. The negotiator compartmentalized the problems and picked the easy one first. The think tank corrected the "flunking out" perception of the subject. This was a reality check that people under stress often do not see. Their stress level is so high that they have tunnel vision and frequently miss the obvious.

10. The negotiator agreed with the subject on many points. In the narrative above, she agreed with the "stupid law," but it was the law and must be obeyed.

Do You Need Three Cars?

A suicidal subject named Chuck called the police on his cell phone to tell them where he was and that he planned to kill himself. He said he was alone in his car, which he described, and had his service revolver with him. Like so many suicidal subjects, they do not realize they are communicating their ambivalence so clearly. He was in his car parked in a vacant industrial area on a Sunday morning. The lot and the buildings were empty. Because it was Sunday morning, the response time was fast. The area was easy to cordon off, and negotiations began over the phone.

N: Can you hear me O.K.?

Chuck: Yeah, I hear you loud and clear.

N: O.K. I am Tim with the West End Police Department. What is going on?

Chuck: My life is over. My wife died a few months ago, I lost my job, I cannot sell our house in this market, and I think I have cancer. (Like most suicidal people, he had a lot of problems. In addition, taken as a whole, he had a heavy burden. So a good tact is to take one issue at a time.)

N: Chuck, are you thinking about killing yourself?

Chuck: That is the only solution.

N: Only solution?

Chuck: Yeah. There is just too much to cope with.

N: That sounds like a lot of bad stuff. I am sorry to hear about your wife. How long were you married?

Chuck: We were together for thirty-five years.

N: Thirty-five years.

Chuck: They were the good times. Now she is gone, and there is no point in my going on.

(As Tim was listening to Chuck, the tactical team was positioning itself and in the process reported the tag number so the intelligence-gathering process began. Accurate intelligence is vital. It is best when other negotiators gather it. They know what kind of information the people on scene need. Just as the tactical team has special intelligence needs, so has the negotiator. By way of example, the negotiator should know whether the subject has a pistol. Obviously, the tactical team wants to know whether it is an automatic or a revolver? What is the caliber?)

N: It sounds like you were really in love.

Chuck: Yes, we were. But she is gone and took my life with her.

N: When did she pass away?

Chuck: Two months ago. Then I lost my job.

N: Lost your job?

Chuck: Yeah. I was working security at the mall, and I fell asleep on the job.

N: Fell asleep?

Chuck: Yeah. I have not been sleeping much since Carole passed away, and I guess it caught up with me. They were overstaffed in security, so they cut the staff by firing me.

N: Just you?

Chuck: Yeah. Without my job, our house will go, as will our cars.

N: How many cars do you have?

Chuck: Three, counting the SUV.

N: That's a lot of cars.

The discussion continued as the negotiator drew Chuck out and compartmentalized his problems. A statement like "Sounds like you have a pretty full plate" shows sympathy, with a follow-up of lets look at the problem of too many cars and discuss what might be done with that one. Stress in a shooting or a suicidal situation is typically accompanied by tunnel vision. Those involved tend not to see logical alternatives. I suggest you or your team select one problem to which there are some solutions. Even if the subject has tried many of your suggestions, the offering of solutions demonstrates your concern. Remember, we negotiate as a team, so while the primary is listening to the subject, others on the team and those in the think tank are working on solutions and alternatives. In this case, the negotiator focused on the cars. Does a single person really need three cars? It turned out that selling two cars or trading them in to the dealer to reduce the payment on the car he kept had not occurred to Chuck. It is not the job of the negotiator to solve all the problems of suicidal people. Many of them have spent their lives creating the mess they are in that cannot be corrected in one discussion. Our job is to delay a fatal act and offer some hope. Many times helping solve one problem does just that. In addition, it delays the suicide because it offers an alternative. The doubt issue can be addressed by a discussion of the Golden Gate Bridge story about those few who survived and said that right after they jumped they changed their mind but it was too late. These approaches and many more are covered in depth in *Psychological Aspects of Crisis Negotiations* (2nd ed.) (Strentz, 2012) and other texts.

It is not our job to solve all of their problems. We should focus on delay, alternatives, and doubt to get them out so a professional can help them through their crisis. However, when a solution seems obvious, common sense says discuss it. We have nothing to lose. Our discussion may provide a solution. It will convey our concern. In this case, Chuck and the negotiator talked about which car to sell. While this discussion was going on, other negotiators contacted the dealer to get a ballpark figure on the value of Chuck's vehicles and lined up the departmental psychologist, who was in the think tank, to talk with Chuck. I know from experience that most psychologists deal with de pressed and suicidal people on a daily basis. That is why most of them have other mental health professionals with whom they can talk to unload their day of depression. As negotiators, we typically draw from our limited experience. Suicide is much too serious a problem for us to rely on personal experience and common sense for a solution. Most departments have mental health professionals available. To do our job more effectively, we must use them.

Chuck surrendered his weapon and was counseled by the department's psychologist, who arranged additional treatment in a "Grief Group" sponsored by a local hospital.

Epilogue

Chuck sold one of his cars and the SUV. He also found a job. A few weeks later, he came by the department to thank the negotiator for getting him through his crisis and told him what he had done to solve his problems. His solutions seem obvious and logical to others. A person under stress often lacks logic and objectivity.

Lessons Learned

1. Active listening skills were used effectively.
2. The crucial question "Are you thinking about killing yourself?" was asked. This question helps clear the air. It provides focus and helps determine whether the subject trusts the negotiator with his feelings.
3. Officers who understood what type of information the negotiator needed gathered intelligence.
4. The negotiator helped the subject focus on one problem at a time. He chose one that he thought they could solve. During this phase, the think tank suggested a field officer contact the car dealer to determine how much each vehicle was worth.
5. Follow-up by mental health is crucial. A lack of follow-up in suicidal callouts all too often leads to a repeat performance.

Man's Best Friend (and a Women's as Well)

Most law enforcement officers who work at a shopping mall focus on thefts and rowdy customers. Because of the frequency of calls to these typically crowded locations, many police and sheriff substations are located at shopping malls. This routine was broken one afternoon during the "Christmas shopping season," when an adult male called the mall and said his mother was suicidal and had driven to the mall with the intent of jumping to her death. He described her and her vehicle. He also knew part of her license number.

While she continued to speak with the caller, the dispatcher immediately notified command and all units of the situation and provided the identifiers she had. The caller said he knew she was at the mall because she told him she was going there to return some decorations so her credit card would be cleared of recent purchases of things she would not need. He identified one of the stores. Although she did not tell him she was going to jump, he was concerned. The tone of her voice and recent behavior triggered an internal alarm. Her husband, who was his father and a retired federal employee, passed away recently. This was her first Christmas without him. She was very depressed over his death. In addition, she was having serious financial problems with the Internal Revenue Service and the Office of Personnel Management. He said he was en route to the mall.

Officers located her vehicle at the top of the mall parking facility. They said the car windows were "cracked open," and there was a small old dog in the car. By prearranged plan, the upper decks of parking facility were closed. Dispatch called her son and advised him of developments. She told him to proceed to the police parking lot at the mall, identify himself, and ask for Sergeant Smith. He said he knew where that lot was and thanked her for the information.

At about that time, other officers responded saying she had already returned the items to one store. The clerk did not know if she was going to other stores, but commented that she did not remember seeing the elderly lady carrying other items. Moments later, officers in the parking facility called to report that an elderly female who matched the description given by the caller was standing near the railing overlooking the mall at a level well above Coroners Height. While one officer reported the find, his partner initiated face-to-face negotiations at a safe distance. Fortunately, both were on the negotiations team. They made the immediate decision not to call her by name.

> NEG: Morning, mam. I am Deputy Jane Jones with the King County Sheriff's Department. Are you O.K?
>
> Female: No answer.
>
> NEG: Mam, are you O.K?
>
> Female: Not really.
>
> NEG: Not really?
>
> Female: No, not really. There is just too much that is too bad and all wrong.
>
> NEG: Can you tell me what is wrong?
>
> Female: There is so much wrong, I do not know where to start.
>
> NEG: It doesn't matter where you start. Just tell me what is wrong.
>
> Female: You work hard all your life. Pay your taxes, do what is right, and obey the law, and all they give you back is a bunch of crap.
>
> NEG: A bunch of crap?
>
> Female: That's what I said. They dish out a bunch of crap or the silent treatment. I don't know which is worse.
>
> NEG: Who is giving you a bunch of crap?
>
> Female: The damn Internal Revenue Service. That's who.
>
> NEG: How is the IRS giving you crap?
>
> Female: You pay your taxes. They cash your check, can't figure out what they did with the money, and demand you pay them again.
>
> NEG: Pay them again? I don't understand.
>
> Female: Of course you don't. You are not the Infernal or is it the Incompetent Revenue Service.

NEG: That is an interesting use of terms. How are they incompetent?

Female: Like I said, they cashed our check, lost our money, and then want me us to pay them again. Month after month, they send threatening letters. Each letter is worse. They add interest, penalties, and threaten to withhold any future refunds . . . and it's all their fault.

NEG: Can you tell me the sequence of events?

Female: Last year my husband made an extra $20,000 doing some consulting work. We sent the IRS some money for taxes in advance and paid bills. When we went to our accountant, he figured we owed more money, about $2,900. I don't recall the exact amount but it was just under $3,000. So we filed our return, and for the first time in our lives, we sent the IRS a check for the money we owed. That was before the deadline in April. My husband passed on in May.

NEG: I am sorry to hear that.

Female: Well in June, I received this letter from IRS saying we owed $2,900, and I better send them a check for that amount plus additional money for interest and penalties. My son helped me go back on the computer and find the cancelled check to IRS. We printed both sides and sent it to them in the envelope they included in their letter. A few weeks later, I got another letter saying I owed them $2,900. It was a form letter. No mention was made of my letter and the copy of the cancelled check I sent. Now it is almost Christmas, and I get letters and more letters with more and more interest and penalties due. I paid my taxes on time. I sent them proof. They are treating me like a crook.

NEG: That is ridiculous. What you are saying is that, because they cannot find where they put your money, they want you to pay your taxes again?

Female: You got that right. The last letter said something about not refunding me any money in the future until this delinquent tax bill was paid. We sent them a check. The check cleared our account. I sent them proof. I am out the money, and they want more. I wrote them a letter saying what if they had sent me a refund, I cashed the check, took the money home, and then lost it. Would they send me another refund? They do not answer letters. They just keep sending them.

NEG: That is certainly putting the ball in their court.

Female: I even went back to our accountant. He is a nice guy. He told me that sooner or later, they will find the money. He told me to ignore the letters. I think he sent them a letter explaining my situation. I don't know. They make me feel like a cheat. A crook. I pay my taxes and do what is right, and all they do is send me threatening letters.

NEG: Well, it seems to me you have done the right thing. You paid your taxes and have contacted your accountant. It is frustrating to just keep getting those stupid letters.

Female: That is just part of the story.

NEG: There's more? (As she told her story, she moved further away from the railing. Therefore, the negotiator did not ask about her intent to commit suicide.)

Female: Yes, there are the fools at the Office of Personnel Management.

NEG: What is the Office of Personnel Management?

Female: I guess you don't know because you don't work for the federal government. They are the people who handle federal retirement.

NEG: Federal retirement.

Female: Yes. Once you retire, like John did from the Department of Justice, the people in OPM figure out how much you should get and send out the monthly check. It took us four months to get our first check, and it was wrong. So John wrote them a letter about that. We heard nothing. The checks just kept coming in the wrong amount. So John wrote registered letters, made phone calls, and left messages. He even went to their web site and sent them an email. They never responded to anything we sent or said. We have a dozen registered letter receipts from the post office, but nothing from them. So, John and I went to our congressman. He wrote a letter and told us he would hear from them in a month. A month later, John called our congressman and was told that it would be thirty working days, not thirty regular days. So that meant about six weeks. Then our congressman called. Actually, it was a nice lady on his staff. She said the matter had been resolved. Well, they lied to her. The checks are still coming in the wrong amount.

(All of this took time, during which her son arrived at the mall. So far the negotiator has not solved any of her problems. That is not her job. Her job, with the help of the think tank and her secondary, is to listen and hope for hooks. So far no hooks, just a lot of justified frustration.)

NEG: I understand why you are upset.

Female: It is just too much. It was tough enough when John was handling all this. I just cannot do it alone.

NEG: Is there anyone who can help? (The negotiator knew about her son from dispatch and her story. Whenever possible, it is best to ask a question to which you already know the answer.)

Female: We have children. Our oldest son lives here. The others are out of state. (She went on to discuss each of their three children, their location, grandchildren, and other family members.)

NEG: You are certainly fortunate to be blessed with such wonderful children. (The decision was made not to tell her about the call from or presence of her son at this time.)

Female: They are wonderful and will be better off without me to burden them.

NEG: Why do you say burden them?

Female: They have their own lives to live and do not need me around, especially with all these problems with IRS and OPM. They are so stupid. That reminds me, I left our dog Autumn in my car. Will you make sure he goes to the SPCA so they can find a good home for him? (This could be a hook.)

NEG: How long have you had Autumn?

Female: John and I got him as a puppy years and years ago. He is twelve.

NEG: Twelve years old.

Female: Yes, he has been around for a long time. We got him as an early warning system and companion. He did both jobs well. Dogs are wonderful, and Autumn deserves a good home. (Now this is definitely becoming a hook. Note she says "we" and "our" when she refers to Autumn. The think tank interpreted this as a sign she was still in mourning.)

NEG: Well, I hate to tell you this, but the SPCA often has problems finding a home for an old dog. I think in dog years, Autumn is in his 70s.

Female: Yes, he is old but very alert and faithful.

NEG: Getting back to the SPCA. You know they try. But again, they do not always succeed.

Female: I am sure they will with Autumn.

NEG: Well, you are betting his life on that. (This phrase came from the think tank.)

Female: What do you mean betting his life?

NEG: Well, after a few weeks or so, they put unadopted dogs down.

Female: Put them down? You mean put them to death?

NEG: Unfortunately, yes.

Female: (Now through her tears.) But Autumn deserves better than that. He is a good dog.

NEG: I am sure he is to you. But to them, he is just another dog.

Female: (More sobs.) (They found the hook. Now how can it be used?) He is not just another dog. He is our Autumn.

NEG: I understand that. I have a dog and love him.

Female: I don't know what to do.

NEG: (It is not our job to solve problems, but to gain time and delay any suicide attempts until a mental health professional can intervene after the incident has been resolved. However, some advice was in order. That advice had been prepared by the think tank that included the department's mental health professional. In this case, he was a social worker.) I think you should move away from that railing and take some time to think this through. You are not alone. I am here to help. Your son is here and wants to talk to you.

Female: My son? You called my son?

NEG: No, he called us. He was concerned about you.

Female: Lots of crying. (She moved away from the railing. The two negotiators moved toward her together and had her sit down in their patrol car.)

Epilogue

Her son was very comforting as was Autumn, who was brought from her car to be by her side. The department social worker followed up and reported back to the negotiator a few weeks later that the IRS wrote her saying they found her check and all was forgiven. (Those are my words. IRS does not forgive. They just stop pestering people.) She was under the care of a medical doctor and responding well to treatment and therapy in a "Grief Group" at her church. OPM remained mute and continued to mail the retirement checks in the wrong amount.

Lessons Learned

1. Her son was a valuable resource. He provided the think tank with valuable information they used to formulate an effective negotiations strategy.
2. The mental health professional helped on scene and then followed up. In my opinion, a mental health follow-up after a suicide attempt is vital. Otherwise issues remain unresolved, and the stage is set for a repeat performance.

3. The think tank was a valuable asset. It coordinated the flow of intelligence and provided, through the secondary, valuable suggestions and recommendations for the primary. They picked up on her use of "our dog" versus "my dog" as an indicator that she was still in mourning.

4. These negotiations certainly achieved a high level of ALS. They are well above the Louisiana State Police goal of 80% listening and 20% talking. As usual, the ALS process identified the hook.

5. The decision not to call her by name was a judgment call. Just because we know something does not mean we must reveal it. Knowing her name could force us to identify her son. During the negotiations, the department did not know the nature of her relationship with her son. So, he was not mentioned until later. It was decided that, should it come up, the negotiator would say that a deputy on routine patrol had identified her.

Countdown to Death

This case was a seven-hour hostage siege that was featured in an NBC Dateline Survivors series titled "Trouble in Paradise." It involved a disgruntled former employee of a Hawaiian firm named Seal Master who returned to his former place of employment at 7:00 a.m. to take revenge on the man who fired him. It is an excellent example of workplace violence and the phenomena titled "Suicide by Cop" (SbC). It demonstrates the effective use of time.

I was not on scene. I taught an advanced hostage negotiations course in Honolulu a few weeks after the incident and learned the details of the siege from them. Before 8:00 a.m. the Honolulu Police Department was called by the owner of Seal Master who told them of the presence of a heavily armed former employee named John Miranda. John was in the company office where he held several people hostage. The owner knew this because he was called by one of the hostages who told him that John Miranda was back seeking revenge and wanted $20,000 from the company. The owner told the police he would get the money and drive to town.

The site of the incident was an industrial park named Sand Island. It is located between the airport and downtown Honolulu. Containment was quickly achieved. The tactical team was in place around and on top of the building. The negotiators were around the corner. The negotiations process began. The negotiators made a phone call to the office and spoke to the subject. He wanted $20,000 and the opportunity to voice his version of his dismissal. He wanted to be interviewed on a local radio station. He clamed he had been discriminated against.

His employer said he had used drugs on the job and had threatened other employees. At age 28, John was a big man at 6'5" and weighed 250 pounds. He had a history of violent confrontations with the Honolulu Police and was a suspected drug user. He had over more than arrests and sixteen convictions for a variety of offenses that ranged from drug use to traffic tickets and assault.

The police immediately began gathering intelligence that included identifying the registered owners of the vehicles in the parking lot. They also obtained floor plans for the office. The problem was that Seal Master made many internal changes that were not yet on file. Employees arriving for work were detained and interviewed. From them it was learned that although people were being held hostage in the office, several others were in other parts of the complex. They based this information on the identity of the owners of cars in the parking lot and their knowledge of those who usually arrived early. The negotiations process went something like the following.

NEG: This is Officer Karen Kaneohe with the Honolulu Police Department. Can you tell me what is going on in there?

SUB: I got these "Haole" bastards, and they are going to pay for firing me. (Haole is pronounced how lee. It is a local derogatory name for non-Hawaiians.)

NEG: They fired you?

SUB: Yeah, for no good reason, and now they are going to pay.

NEG: Pay?

SUB: Yeah. They are going to pay me $20,000, and I want to go on the radio and tell everyone what is going on.

NEG: $20,000. That is a lot of money.

SUB: They can afford it. They owe me.

NEG: They owe you?

SUB: Yeah. They fired me, and now it's pay back time.

NEG: Why did they fire you?

SUB: Because I am a local boy. They kept everyone else. I want to go on the radio and tell everyone what they did.

(Arrangements were made for a local radio station to interview him. The agreement was for the interview to occur, but not to be played until he came out, a euphemism for surrender. The station agreed. During the interview and negotiations, John said over and over that he was not going to prison, and the situation was going to end in violence. His words were "In a gun bang.")

SUB: I can't find my interview.

NEG: Remember, the agreement was to play it after you came out.

SUB: That's a lie.

(Members of John's family arrived. He had twelve brothers and sisters by several fathers who recorded pleas to him to surrender. He refused to listen to them.)

(A check of owners of vehicles in the parking lot revealed that one car was registered to John's girlfriend with whom he had been living and with whom he had a stormy relationship. She was missing. Neighbors had not seen her, and she had not been at work for about a week.)

(In the course of the morning, he continued to rant. He fired a shot out the window from his sawed-off shotgun. He also shot one employee in the leg. This was the person he blamed for his termination. The man fell to the floor bleeding. Then John had to use the bathroom. He took his hostages with him. However, the man he shot remained on the floor. When they returned to the office, the wounded hostage was gone. He had crawled and managed to escape out a window. He was immediately transported to a local hospital. He survived.)

(John then used duct tape to secure his sawed-off shotgun to the neck of one hostage and secure the trigger area of the weapon to his right hand. He exited the building with the secured hostage and two other hostages. He paraded them around the parking lot. Elements of the tactical team entered the building and rescued the hidden hostages. They also locked the door.)

(The tactical team in the parking lot could not shoot because they feared that shooting John would cause him to fall, and in the process, he would pull the trigger of his shotgun and kill the hostage. During this demonstration of contempt and bravado, John noticed the muzzle of the shotgun was no longer taped to the neck of his hostage and pointing to his head. The humidity of Hawaii and all the pushing and shoving caused the muzzle to loosen and move down to his shoulder. He sent one hostage back to get more tape. When the former hostage entered the building, he was grabbed by officers and not allowed to leave. In the confusion, his other unrestrained hostage escaped. This left John and the hostage with the shotgun now much more loosely taped to his neck in the parking lot.)

(John told his hostage to count backward from sixty. He said for everyone to hear that when he got to zero, he was going to blow his head off. His hostage refused to count. John began counting. The tactical team interrupted his counting over and over by telling him to surrender. He lost track of his counting and began again. During this exchange, his last hostage noticed the loose shotgun was now bouncing off his trapezoid, not his neck. When John got to thirteen, he turned and began wrestling John for the weapon. It was a "David and Goliath" struggle. However, he was able to move the weapon away from his head. John was able to pull the trigger and fire one round. The tactical team opened fire and shot John several times. He died at the scene. An autopsy revealed numerous drugs in his system to include cocaine, met amphetamine, and marijuana. His hostage survived. I suspect he suffered some loss of hearing.)

Lessons Learned

1. One can consider this case an example of workplace violence and/or SbC. In either case, the Honolulu Police Department used time to defuse and confuse the hostage taker.

2. There is an old saying that God helps those who help themselves. In this case the hostage helped himself by wrestling for the loose shotgun and in so doing gave the tactical team the opportunity to shoot the subject without hitting his hostage.
3. Intelligence gathered on vehicles in the parking lot identified the auto of the subject's girlfriend. Based on interviews with neighbors, the police suspected foul play. Her body was found a few days later in a shallow grave.
4. Family members were interviewed to gather intelligence and plead with their brother to surrender. John refused to listen to them. However, the department made a reasonable effort to use them and to negotiate a peaceful resolution.
5. Time was used well to gather intelligence and also cause the shotgun to be worked loose from the hostage's head.

Summary

It is clear that traditional hostage situations are no longer the most common callouts for negotiation teams. Research done by the FBI substantiates this reality. Suicidal situations and lone barricaded gunmen now represent the majority of calls for negotiation teams service. It is therefore incumbent on law enforcement and corrections to train for these sieges. This training is usually free and readily available from local "Suicide Hot Lines." In fact, many departments already train with this resource and provide negotiators the opportunity to "work a hot line shift" in place of their regular shift with their department. This training and experience is invaluable because it provides officers with the opportunity to use their listening skills. In my experience, law enforcement and correctional officers are adept at reading body language of those they interview. However, their skills are not so finely honed when it comes to listening to what is and is not being said. Hot line training and experience can easily and effectively remedy this gap in expertise. I speak from experience. Mine was.

References

Chelsea Hayes v. County of San Diego. (2011). 658 F. 3rd 867.
Dalfonzo, V. A., & Romano, S. J. (2003, October). Negotiation Position Papers: A Tool for Crisis Negotiators. *FBI Law Enforcement Bulletin,* pp. 27–29.

Noesner, G. (2010). Stalling for Time, Random House, New York.

Strentz, T. (2012). *Psychological aspects of crisis negotiations* (2nd ed.). Boca Raton, FL: CRC Press.

Chapter 6

IN SUMMATION

The legendary Spanish-American philosopher George Santayana said, "Those who do not study their history are condemned to repeat it." That has been the theme of this book and is the focus of this summation. In law enforcement and corrections, when we repeat mistakes, people die, careers end prematurely, and we are successfully sued. As negotiators, we must learn from those who have gone before. Too err is human but make your own mistakes and do not repeat those of others.

Throughout this book, I have listed lessons learned after each negotiation with the intent of introducing some common sense and court decisions into our life-saving efforts and this process. Remember the old adage, when emotions increase, reason decreases. That is why we use a negotiations team rather than a lone representative of our agency. I recall one prolonged incident when one emotional commander kept saying about the subject's reneging on promises, "He can't do that to me. Who does he think he is, lying to the . . . ?" His emotions took charge and in my view led to a premature and unnecessary assault. Many people died whose lives could have been spared.

As negotiators, there are times when a subject does things to upset us, pull our chain, or otherwise play games with us. Again, this is why we have a team to support our efforts. A subject may be more intelligent than one of us but not smarter than all of us. In addition, teams help defuse stress and certainly make better decisions collectively than any of us can make on our own. Certainly we have learned the importance of recording negotiations so our think tank can listen to what was said and in so doing assist the negotiation in her or his efforts to stay on track, understand layered messages, and help the subject help himself out of the siege without the unnecessary loss of human life.

The fairly recent innovation from the Crisis Negotiations Unit at Quantico titled "Negotiation Position Papers" is an excellent idea and long overdue. In my experience, I have said all too often, "That makes so much sense. Why did I not think of that?" Well, I still cannot answer that question, but I have attempted to include tactics and techniques that make sense so this generation of crisis negotiators can learn from those of us who have gone before and learned too many lessons the hard way.

Blessed are the peacemakers for they shall be called the children of God (Matthew 5:9). I do not believe that we as negotiators have a corner on the market of making or keeping the peace. However, experience has taught me that of all those responding to hostage and suicide sieges, we typically play the leading role in this life-saving process.

References

King James, Matthew 5:9.

Santayana, G. (1905). In J. Bartlett (1960) *Book of Familiar Quotations* (p. 703). Boston: Little, Brown.

NAME INDEX

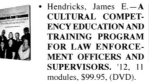

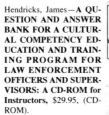

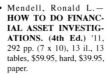
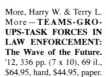

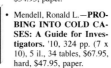